Endo

We live in a world entangled in the web of past failures and drowning in the sorrow that it brings. While society develops new terms to diagnose the problems, people search temporary medications or pain relievers to cope with another day, but missing the permanent fix.

God Speaks to the Weary Heart is a book that brings hope through the personal experience of one who has found the path to healing through application of spiritual truths and faith in God.

On the heels of a dramatic and life changing encounter with the Lord, author Chris Kline broke away from her worldly past and boldly entered the ministry, applying the principles of faith that had brought her own deliverance. The anointing upon her ministry is evidenced by the response at the altars and the testimony of people whose lives have been eternally changed.

God Speaks to the Weary Heart brings practical insight to biblical principles, amplified by the personal experiences of author, Chris Kline. To those who are battle-weary and on the precipice of giving up, here is a book that will give you hope and make you smile. As a pastor, I recommend this book to people who recognize a call to leadership, but struggle with the course. If you recognize the problems and need help with the Answer, read on. Chris Kline found the path to victory and so can you.

—Pastor Phil Derstine,
Christian Retreat, Bradenton, FL.

We live in a day in which a great number of Christians have been hurt by other Christians.

This is not new. Christians have been doing this to one another throughout the ages. And they have always done it in the name of the Lord. Nonetheless, this generation has given us teachings that have justified the cruelty of one Christian inflicting pain on another.

We are fallen people. We should expect this kind of conduct, this kind of pain, to fall into our lives at the hand of other believers. Such conduct has been true in the past; it is true now. The kind of pain inflicted by one believer on another will continue throughout all coming generations. Our problem is, there have been few books and virtually no ministry which have addressed this subject. Further, we live in a day when the understanding of the cross may be at an all time low in the history of Protestant Christianity.

Chris Kline has added to the small number of books that can help to comfort and heal. She has gone through some deep and unique waters, yet managed to come out on the other side with a testimony that will be of comfort and meaning to believers.

I applaud the book. We need more books that deal with the subject of suffering and injustice.

—Gene Edward, author,
A Tale of Three Kings

GOD
Speaks to the Weary Heart

Chris Kline

Bridge-Logos *Publishers*

North Brunswick, New Jersey 08902 USA

God Speaks to the Weary Heart
by Chris Kline
Copyright © 1999
by Bridge-Logos Publishers
Library of Congress Card Catalog Number: 99-90644
International Standard Book Number: 0-88270-778-7

Published by:
Bridge-Logos *Publishers*
1300 Airport Road, Suite E
North Brunswick, NJ 08902

For further information about Chris Kline and her ministry, please contact:

Chris Kline Ministries
183 Denmark Drive
Ellenton, FL 34222
e-mail: healedhearts@aol.com

Acknowledgments

Since about three months after I came to know the Lord, I have held a microphone and shared my faith —sometimes to a few, sometimes to thousands. At times, I've shared God's truth based on the testimonies, sermons and books of others, long before I personally learned a specific lesson. After seventeen years, it's hard to remember which were my own insights and which were those of others.

Plato had this to say about borrowing others' thoughts: "Bees cull their several sweets from this flower and that blossom, here and there where they can find them, but themselves after make the honey which is purely their own." What you will read here is purely my own. Eventually, I had to apply personally all that I had cultivated. In some cases, I didn't do it very well. But fortunately, God teaches truths not only *before* as prevention and *during* as solution but also *after* as consolation.

With that in mind, I'd like to acknowledge the contributions of:

• Youth With A Mission, which provided acceptance and love and a sense of purpose, as well as an outlet to see God use me.

• All the ministers who graciously gave me the opportunity to preach from their pulpits and touch the lives of their people as they also touched mine. In the end, they have become part of my spiritual inheritance.

• My good friend and colleague Kurt Fox. Many times, we exchanged revelations, added our own insights and then preached them! He prayed me through the roughest time of my life, and I can never thank him enough.

• And, of course, the Lord, who didn't give up on me and who brought promise out of disaster. In the final months I spent writing this book, He sent two people to help me complete it: a preacher named Robbie Hayes and an obedient servant named Richard Peirce.

Table of Contents

Foreword ix
Introduction xiii

1. Too Many Hurts 1
2. Out of Captivity 9
3. When Time Doesn't Heal 15
4. Freedom from Deception 21
5. Peace through Forgiveness 27
6. Never Give Up 35
7. Devoured by the Church 41
8. Costly Betrayal 45
9. When Hope Is Gone 51
10. Erasing Old Tapes 59
11. The Spoken Word of God 67
12. Looking at the Enemy 77
13. The God of the Bad Times 87
14. Waiting for the Crown 93
15. Relinquishing Our 'Rights' 99
16. Anointed—Again—for Ministry 103
17. Death of a Vision 107
18. He'll Do It Again 111
19. Revival of Joy 117
20. The God of Second Chances 129
21. A Weary Heart 137
22. Finding God in Crisis 143

23. Passing through the Deep 149

24. Bless This Mess 155

25. Hearing from God 165

26. Overcoming Rejection 175

27. Needing a Reprieve 185

28. Ambassadors of Reconciliation 191

29. Painless Witnessing 199

30. The Road Home 209

31. Already Married 221

Foreword

Back in 1993, a national Christian magazine assigned me to interview a little-known evangelist who lived nearby. Chris Kline had been defrauded of nearly a half-million dollars by another evangelist who was well-known among the magazine's readers, and I was to interview her for a news story about the lawsuit.

But after the story was in the hands of the magazine editor, I began to realize that a larger story—that of Chris's impact on my life—was only beginning to unfold.

She called one day and invited me to hear her preach during the coming weekend at a church fifteen miles away. Sunday turned out to be one of those rainy, chilly, end-of-winter days typical of the Delmarva peninsula, the kind of day that makes you want to sleep in under a warm down comforter. Driving to the service, I thought, this better be worth it. After all, if I had been going to my own church closer to home, I could have slept a few minutes longer.

Once Chris began to preach, though, I knew it was going to be an unusual service. No doubt about it, she was a powerful, anointed preacher. I was completely unprepared for the impact her words would have on me that day. As Chris gave the altar call, I found myself doubled over by the power of the Holy Spirit. The Lord was clearly beckoning me to go forward for emotional healing.

I didn't want to go. I told myself that I didn't want Chris to think I had gone forward out of courtesy to her. In reality, I didn't want her—or anyone else—to know how spiritually needy I was after a full twenty years of walking with the Lord. Mine was a weary heart in need of reviving.

Somehow, the Spirit of God broke through my resistance and led me to the front of the church, which was packed with men and women who had been profoundly touched by Chris' message. By the time Chris reached me in the prayer line, the Holy Spirit had already spoken words to my spirit that erased the pain and shame that had haunted me for years.

Shortly after that day, our family moved to Florida, and Chris moved to Virginia. We had seemingly gone our separate ways. Several years later, however, I received an unexpected call from Chris—who had also moved to Florida. As we talked about the events in our lives that had taken place in the intervening years, I learned that the man who had defrauded her was still in a prominent position of ministry. What struck me most during our conversation, though, was Chris's total lack of bitterness toward him—or toward God.

Here was a woman who lived by faith, ministering each weekend in the smaller churches that dot the landscape of the East Coast, at times for a love offering that barely covered her travel expenses—knowing all the while that the riches that once were hers were squandered by someone she trusted. Like me, you probably know people who have walked away from God and lived their lives in spiritual isolation and bitterness for reasons far less significant.

But that's not Chris. In recent years, when her own heart began to grow weary, she never abandoned God or her commitment to serve Him—even when it looked as if she might have to give up her public ministry. Throughout that time, God continued to use her, all the while teaching her the deep lessons of emotional healing that would so powerfully affect the lives of those who heard her preach.

Has your heart grown weary? May you discover, as I did, that hearing—and heeding—what the Lord has to say through Chris Kline is by all means worth it!

—Marcia Ford
News Editor for *Christian Retailing*

Introduction

A few years ago, I was invited by an old boyfriend to attend the kickoff concert for the Rolling Stones' world tour. My friend has worked with the Stones for several decades, and I've stayed in touch with him over the years. He's known me both before and since my conversion to Christ.

As an itinerant evangelist—and a single woman—I wouldn't normally consider attending a Stones concert. But when my friend called, I jumped at the opportunity to go—not only because I wanted to see him but also because I had some follow-up work to do with Mick Jagger. Several years earlier I had sent Mick a copy of my first book, *A Brilliant Deception,* in which I described some of the experiences I had with the Stones in the '70s. I wanted to find out if Mick had read the book, which detailed my conversion and the events leading up to it.

Following the concert, which was predictably demonic, I was among a select few invited to attend a private party for the Stones at the Ritz Hotel in Washington, D.C. After being waved through a number of checkpoints, my sisters and I apparently passed muster and were ushered into the ballroom.

Most of the people in the room were strangers, people that the band and its entourage would probably never see again. Yet everyone was friendly and genuinely interested in who you were and how you managed to get into this elite party. Jagger himself got up from his dinner table and shook hands with anyone bold enough to approach him.

The party felt like a family celebration, and Mick made everyone feel welcome. I asked him if he'd read the book I sent; with a grin, Mick answered, "Oh, yes, I started it." Not to be deterred or intimidated, I smiled and said, "Well, you need to finish it."

As I walked around making small talk, I compared the atmosphere at the party to that which permeates the many church socials I attend. I noticed a disconcerting difference. At the Stones' party, everyone seemed to be talking to everyone else. In the church, I often see people sitting alone, and no one seems to notice.

That feeling of isolation is certainly not limited to socials. In churches throughout the country, on any given Sunday visitors have to find their way through a trail of dust as their brethren fly out the door heading for a local restaurant. And those same visitors are left to decide if they will ever want to return to that same church.

It just doesn't make sense, does it? The Stones and their entourage embrace a room full of strangers, most of whom they'll never see again, while we in the church keep at arm's length the very people we'll spend eternity with.

Why are so many of us reluctant to "reach out and touch someone"? And if we won't even say hello to a stranger in church, how likely is it that we'll do much witnessing?

While there are many reasons why we find it difficult to emotionally embrace others, I'd like to suggest that a critical reason has its roots in one of the most pervasive problems in the church today. In my own life, and in the lives of countless others I've ministered to from the pulpit since 1986, I've seen it happen: We've simply lost heart. Sad !!

For years, we've prayed for something specific, something that we believe God promised to us, something good and pure and certainly within His ability to accomplish. But it has not come forth. Our faith has been eroded, our once-bright fire has dimmed to a flicker. We've lost heart.

We shouldn't be surprised. Jesus Himself warned about the danger of losing heart. Just look at the parable of the persistent widow in Luke 18.

The parable implies that if a godless judge would grant the widow's request because of her persistence, then our just God will by all means answer the pleas of "his chosen ones, who cry out to him day and night" (verse 7). Jesus implies that if we want to see God move on our behalf, we might have to wear Him down the way the widow did the judge.

And He shows that while waiting to see God respond to our requests, it's feasible that we could lose heart. He concludes the illustration by embedding a warning in one of His usual thought-provoking questions: "When the Son of Man comes, will he find faith on the earth?" (verse 8).

What is it you have been waiting to see God bring about? Is it a vision, a dream, justice, prosperity? Is it something selfless, such as the desire to see a loved one saved; restoration in a relationship? Is it a healing for someone whose life is draining your hope?

Son/
Justin

If the answer has been delayed for many months, will you still have faith when the Son of Man comes, or will you have lost heart? Instead of expectant joy and belief, will He find shades of hopelessness, disappointment, dullness—a heart that has become stony again?

If you lost heart as you sought your answer, all the other things that God wanted you to believe for also never came forth. The reason? Your prayer life was stymied as you waited for the answers to a handful of specific prayers, and you didn't ask for anything else. All around you angels waited to go forth and minister according to your prayers, but no orders were given because no prayers were sent.

As the last days rapidly approach, God is bringing about revival. From the largest churches in the inner cities to the smallest congregations in the corn fields of Iowa, a passion is stirring the hearts of God's children. Many believe that through this awakening, God is preparing us for the endtime harvest of non-believers who will come to us for answers when the world system collapses. But what has to happen to His saints first? Why do they need stirring up? And what does revival have to do with losing heart?

I believe God is sending revival to all who have tasted of His heavenly nature—even those whose hearts have become numb over the years. Ministers and laypeople alike must rekindle their relationships with Jesus. But how do you do it when you're running on empty? You'd be surprised to see what God can do to fill you back up.

In many circles, the term *revival* is equated with a series of special services designed to draw the unchurched into God's kingdom. So we schedule a week of meetings, bring in a fiery evangelist to pitch salvation and watch while he preaches to the saved congregation. The following week, it's back to business as usual—waiting for God to come through for *me*.

As Scripture points out, the Israelites became weary waiting for the Lord. They moaned, "So when is He coming?" And so, sadly, many of them stopped looking.

It's no different today. It's not so much that we've stopped looking for His glorious return, but we've suspended the activity of believing God for the supernatural because we don't see "His coming" in the things we've sought.

We are commanded to "direct [our] hearts into God's love and Christ's perseverance" (2 Thess. 3:5). But to the weary child of God—no matter how mature in Christ—this becomes increasingly difficult after years of disappointment, injustice, confusing guidance and unanswered prayers.

We judge as complacent many who sit in church week after week numb to the things of God. They've lost their vitality; they've given up trying. They experienced the power of God when they were saved and He healed the scars from their former lives, but now they need to see that He can heal the scars from their new life as well. Guilt and condemnation stand in the way, however.

That powerful pair is overwhelming and destructive for the believer who thinks his numbness will cause God to spit him out of His mouth—if the church doesn't do it first. By and large, the church doesn't tolerate those who are weak in faith even though we are commanded to restore one in gentleness lest we too fall (Gal. 6:1). Instead, we respond in ways that send the child of God fleeing to whatever will mend their weary heart.

What causes a devoted servant of the Lord to lose heart, to bring him or her to the point that they just don't care anymore? Guilt, hopelessness and shame slither in to replace love, joy and hope. Instead of contentment with thanksgiving and a sense of destiny, resentment and disillusionment prompt the servant to cry, "God, when are You coming? I can't wait any longer!" Unfulfilled visions and shattered dreams have left us gun shy to believe for more.

As a result, many saints no longer feel special and set apart. We lost that sense of blessing. We've been wounded in the most vulnerable place, our heart. To cope, we went searching for any sort of salve that would provide comfort and keep us going.

We ran from one conference to another, seeking any speaker who was anointed and promised to give us "more of God and His fire." And yet in our homes, in our silence, we still waited for God to come, to show Himself by bringing a *yes!* to those things we hoped for.

The Bible is a living book, a book about truth, about real life, real people, real struggles—and real words from the Son of our living God. The parables Jesus told still speak the truth today.

God came to our biblical brethren in a variety of ways, just as He still comes to us. The victories, failures and shortcomings of our spiritual ancestors weren't documented for our entertainment, curiosity or judgment. Neither are the experiences you'll discover in the following pages. I don't share my ups and downs, and those of countless people I've ministered to, for the benefit of the idly curious. I do so because through them, God has revealed truth. And truth applies to anyone.

Several years ago I served as vice president of the ministerial association in Crisfield, Maryland. Our meetings often focused on the struggles not only in the personal lives of the pastors but also in the lives of their churches. As an unmarried traveling evangelist, I couldn't identify with all their challenges but I had heard similar stories for years.

A year before I left Crisfield, a Baptist pastor assumed a new post in town and joined our group. When he arrived, he was on top of the world. Over the following year, his once-joyous disposition became calloused. His wife didn't like Crisfield, his children rebelled, people gossiped about him, board members tried to usurp his leadership and he had financial burdens.

Recently I spoke with the former president of our ministerium and was saddened to learn that my Baptist friend's second year in Crisfield was even worse than the first one. After years as a stalwart Christian, his faith had crumbled. The final straw was the death of his son in a traffic accident, causing him to question God's love and sovereignty. Because his faith and hope in God had diminished, he felt like a hypocrite. He left the church, the town and the ministry altogether.

As I've traveled and preached over the years, I've heard the secret stories of other ministers who also became faithless and weary. Like some men of faith in the Bible, they too wanted to die. They still preached dynamic sermons that touched the lives of the people, but once they arrived back at home the emptiness and numbness were ever-present.

The truths God has revealed to me are applicable to anyone who has stopped to ask, "Where did my joy go? What happened to my faith, my vision? How do I get my first love back?"

I dedicate this book to all those who carry the same kind of secret, those who through trials and tragedies have grown weary and fainted. The good news, my friend, is that you are not alone. And remember, if you are among those who have lost heart and fainted, your eyes will open again. Fainting is temporary!

Lord, show me in this book
& you wad the Bible
what I need to see!
Open my eyes God!
Amen

One

Too Many Hurts

"The righteous cry out, and the LORD hears them;
he delivers them from all their troubles. The LORD is
close to the brokenhearted and saves those
who are crushed in spirit."
—Psalm 34:17-18

No doubt some of you remember a song that asked, "What becomes of the brokenhearted?"

Look around you, and you'll see the answer. People everywhere grope after "things" to replace the lost ingredients of their heart—hope, joy, love and purpose. Millions are enslaved to the comforts and habits they've acquired to relieve the pain and grief that has smothered all desire to press on. Whether it's manifested in obvious abuses such as drug use or alcoholism, or in the seeming innocence of eating, shopping or spending hours in front of the TV, man's innate need to try to fix himself is evident.

1

From mansions in Beverly Hills to remote tribes in Africa, people find stimulants to help them deal with their lives. Coca leaves in South America, kava from the South Pacific, Prozac from the local pharmacy—humans rebel against emotional discomfort and will take whatever substance helps them cope.

When our hearts are broken, we sense an onslaught of grief that causes a pain near our hearts that we can actually feel. Man's most common antidote to that pain is to harden his heart so it won't hurt so much. How does one do that? It's easy, it's natural and it's human.

For too many, their hopes and dreams of love, security and happiness have never materialized. For others, those same dreams did materialize—and were later shattered. They ended up weary, and they lost heart.

Those of us who are believers share a special kind of heartache. It's the kind that pierces our faith when our seemingly God-ordained endeavors come to a grinding halt. Mistrust and confusion snuff out our vision and desire to press on.

But finding relief in the church can be a challenge. Finding kindred spirits and genuine fellowship in the church is even more difficult. Often, those in the pastorate or the church's inner circle (which nearly every church has to some extent) have no idea that some of their sheep are devouring the rest of the flock, sending the wounded out the back door.

Yes, God's mercies are new every day, but so are the hassles of life and the people who cause them. *"Even my close friend, whom I trusted, he who shared my bread, has lifted up his heel against me" (Ps. 41:9).* That's what the psalmist wrote about Jesus centuries before He lived on earth. The psalmist knew all about betrayal, and he knew that no one, not even Jesus Himself, was immune to it.

Those we have loved or admired, whether wittingly or not, have spurned us, leaving us calloused, hardened and disillusioned. Over time, fresh insults cause unhealed wounds to reappear, and often those we love pay for it by our actions.

One of the quickest routes to a weary heart and a broken spirit comes in the form of rejection from someone of the opposite sex. For highly sensitive people, the mere memory of being spurned by a first crush can have a haunting effect.

The degradation of divorce shatters the spirits of many a man or woman who loved and trusted and gave themselves in intimacy to another, only to have the relationship destroyed. Divorce is a trauma to your spirit like no other. It wreaks havoc on who you are and on your sense of God's destiny in your life.

Parents do and say things in anger only to find out years later that their words and actions had a crippling effect. Their children have grown up with negative memories that formed a negative sense of acceptance that resulted in negative behavior patterns—and the parents wonder what went wrong. I regularly meet adults who still spew bitterness because of something their parents said in a moment of frustration or anger. An angry word was deposited in their spirit and tagged along with them for years.

Of course, children contribute their own brand of grief in their desire to have their own way. Rebellion through actions and words has brought untold heartache to many a parent. The sin of selfishness inherent in all of us ripples to the surface even at the earliest age.

Not too long ago, my mother shared with me my first complete sentence. Apparently, I shook my tiny fist in her face and screamed, "I hate you!" I have always loved my mother, but on that day she probably didn't give me what I wanted. I hurt my mother deeply, because even at that young age my sin nature was revealing its ugly reality.

All of us have to deal with traumas, betrayals and unexpected tragedies. The injustice brought about by the sin and choices of other people leaves us victims with a wounded spirit. All of these arrows that stab us over time aid in crushing our inner man. Once your inner man is crushed, you can't fix it, no matter how hard you try. Only a supernatural touch from Jesus Himself can heal the spiritual man—and only when forgiveness has been extended to the offender.

But too many hurts harden the heart, and often when you're most in need of God's touch your heart is too hard to absorb it. The numbness prohibits penetration.

When we reach this point, those of us who believe in God's love and sovereignty face some problematic questions: Can I still trust Him? If God loves me, why didn't He do something to prevent this injustice? If He is sovereign, why did He allow this injustice? Why didn't He prevent those things that have brought me so much grief?

The danger here is that we may end up doing exactly what the psalmist warns us not to do: We "... *sit in the seat of mockers" (Ps. 1:1).* Even without verbalizing it, we begin to scoff at God. After all, if He is governing the situations of my life why didn't He stop the traumatic events in the first place?

many people ask this. —mostly non-believers

4

Deep inside of us is a defense mechanism that clicks on automatically to help us handle pain, rejection and hurt. All of us have it, and all of us use it. It's called sin. In my heart and yours is a storehouse of variables we can pull out when we need to cope with what others have done to us. We can pull out hatred, anger, resentment, bitterness and vengeance, among many other sins in our storehouse. We can hold a grudge as long as we can. We use these and other evils to ease our pain. It's normal and it's human, but it's also un-Christlike and unhealthy.

After being hurt so many times, our hearts become darkened and the love of God that was originally shed there at the new birth has less chance of expressing itself. Many a saint has become bankrupt in the love department. Over the years, we have given and given and given. We've gone the extra mile, turned the other cheek and suffered much rejection and alienation from those we tried to lead to Christ. All of this adds up, and as a result, when we go to church there isn't much love left to give to another member, much less a stranger.

I'm a visitor in many unfamiliar churches, over the weekends. Until I get up to speak, most people don't know who I am. All too often, the greeter at the door hands me a bulletin while he looks at the floor. I'll look someone square in the face and offer a cheery, "Hello," simply to have them say nothing and keep walking. What's worse, sometimes the person turns away before I can even get out my, "Hello."

What has happened to us that has made us afraid to make eye contact? Have we lost our ability to at least be socially polite? Haven't we read our Bibles? Heb. 13:2 tells us, *"Do not forget to entertain strangers, for by so doing some people have entertained angels without knowing it."*

5

We're like a Dalmatian tied to a fence by a sidewalk. He's checking out the neighborhood and everybody in it. Now God has added a creative feature to a dog that lets you know when he's happy and wants to be your friend: He wags his tail.

Along come some children. The sound of their high-pitched giggles brings the dog to attention, eager for company. His tail is in a full-blown wag. These kids aren't partial to Dalmatians, and as they hurry by, one boy bops the dog on the head and laughs, seeking approval from his peers.

The dog is a little confused. After all, isn't he man's best friend? Along come some more kids. The dog is slightly cautious, a little skeptical, but willing to try again. He sets his tail in motion but not with the same enthusiasm. These kids are full of malicious intent, so they poke some of the dots on the dog and saunter away.

Then comes another boy. The dog begins to expect the worst. He sits on his tail so it won't wag and expose his vulnerability—just like some of us who don't want to reach out anymore. We sit and wait to see if it's worth the effort. @ me

Now this boy is carrying a burger, and our canine friend can't help but smell the beefy aroma. Out comes the tail as the dog hopes for one small bite. Sporting a devilish grin—and remembering all the times his older brother jerked him around—the boy offers the burger to the dog and then gobbles it down himself as he stands just beyond the reach of the leash.

Finally, Mr. Jones comes hobbling up the sidewalk holding tightly to his solid-oak cane. Mr. Jones is afraid of dogs because his limp was caused by an infected dog bite years earlier. He glares at the dog, who now looks skeptical and judgmental, with his lip curled slightly for effect. Mr. Jones decides to get the dog before the dog gets him and slams the cane into the pup's rib cage. To make matters worse, he tells everyone about the nasty dog up the street that got what it deserved.

From the dog's point of view, it doesn't matter who he meets in the future, because his negative opinion of humans is cemented in his emotions. The dog—who was never spiteful before—now treats everybody with contempt, suspicion and, of course, judgment.

Sad.

Many of us in the church have ended up like that dog. People have bopped us on the head, poked some of our dots, bad-mouthed us and offered a loving relationship only to yank it away without warning. Ask yourself this question: Does my tail wag like it used to? If it doesn't, trust me—you're not alone. The question now becomes: How can Jesus ever fix me?

Two

Out of Captivity

*"For look, the wicked bend their bows; they set their
arrows against the strings to shoot from
the shadows at the upright in heart"*
—*Psalms 11:2*

Like me, you've no doubt made some decisions
based entirely on your idea of what would work best.
You thought it out and made your choice according to
what seemed to be logical, productive and suitable to
bring good results, then it backfired. Something
unforeseen happened, and there was nothing you could
do about it. It was too late. You thought, "If only I
could go back in time and do things differently . . . "
I've had my share of those times!   *me too!*

My first months on the mission field were exciting,
challenging and usually uncomfortable. For weeks we
slept in tents or on a mat on the floor of a hut. Finally,
we went to a different island in the Samoan chain, but
this time we would live in a large house with bedrooms

9

and beds. However, only one student would get a private room. As we drew straws to determine who the fortunate one would be, I fervently prayed. My prayer was answered—I got the private room! That night, however, I was too comfortable and couldn't fall asleep. I tossed and turned in my nice, soft bed trying to relax, but nothing worked. Then I remembered that I had a leftover peanut butter and jelly sandwich in my purse, and I figured a full stomach would help me sleep. In the darkness, I reached over to the chair where I had placed my purse and fumbled around until I found the sandwich, all neatly wrapped and still soft.

Carefully, I removed the plastic wrap and charged in with a huge bite. Suddenly I felt a tingling sensation all over my mouth and up my nose. "What in the world is that?" I said out loud. I ran across the room, flicked the light on and looked down at the sandwich. Much to my horror I saw hundreds of ants scurrying around the bread and on my hands. Suddenly I realized that was what I was feeling all over my face and in my nose— not to mention the ones in my mouth and headed south down my throat.

I ran to the sink and cleaned myself up, half in shock and half laughing at the opposite effect this was having on my attempts to fall asleep. Obviously, I was now wide awake. I got back in bed, ready to do battle with my heavenly Father, who I figured was duty-bound to save me from anything so disgusting. After all, I was on His mission field! I was also very naive in the things of God.

Lying there, I conjured up my best praying sigh. "God, why didn't You warn me? Why didn't You tell me to turn the light on?" Deep inside, without a hint of sarcasm, I heard, "You never asked Me." He reminded me that I hadn't said grace, either. I finally fell asleep, with no permanent damage done and a great story to tell at the breakfast table the next day.

Later the following day we held a carnival for the villagers, and I was in charge of the games. I decided to let the boys have a frog race. After carefully tending to 25 frogs the night before—and warning the boys to do the same—I supervised the race and then found myself stuck with all those frogs. I hit upon a bright idea and shouted, "The first boy who gets his frog to the shore wins a prize!" I assumed the boys would run with their frogs, but to my horror they threw them. After all the care I had taken to see that the frogs weren't hurt, I now watched in complete shock as these helpless little creatures went sailing through the air.

We simply can't control all the circumstances or the people in our lives. Ants attack us at night, and kids do unexpected things. When we're newly saved, we find it even more difficult to accept the hardships that come our way. Why didn't God warn me about the ants? Why didn't He give those boys better sense? What we all need to realize is that behind the scenes of our lives is an unseen enemy whose sole purpose is to ruin us, and this perpetrator has known you for a very long time.

A similar incident happened in the Garden of Eden. As we all know, there were two trees there, the tree of life and the tree of knowledge of good and evil.

Eve knew she was not to eat from the tree of knowledge of good and evil. God did not want her deciding for herself what was right and wrong, based on what seemed OK to her. But she listened to the demonic voice of Satan, who convinced her that it would be all right to disobey. Through her disobedience, she was cut off from the life of God.

11

Her children and her children's children—and that includes us—would now be born cut off from the life of God, dead in their sins (Col. 2:13). We would follow the ways of the world and walk according to the prince of the power of the air (Eph. 2:2), and we would be born slaves to the powers of darkness. Satan could hold us captive to do his will (2 Tim. 2:26). Demons could manipulate and even infiltrate people. They owned us, and in a mysterious way, they could affect our hearts and minds. They set out to crush us. As the Bible states, *"The whole world is under the control of the evil one"* *(1 John 5:19).*

If Satan is able to hold us captive to do his will even for a moment, then certainly he has held others captive and used them to hurt us. Most people, including Christians, have no idea how often the unseen forces use them as slaves to do their evil work.

In the Amazon a certain species of ants regularly captures other ants and take them and their eggs back to their colonies to use as slave labor. When the ant eggs hatch, the baby ants come out and begin to do ant stuff. They were born into slavery, and they spend their whole lives doing everything for their captor. They are slaves, and they don't know it. As Christians, especially those who have grown up in the church and heard about God their entire lives, we need to understand that our track record in church is irrelevant to salvation. We also need to dispel the belief, often propagated by well-meaning evangelists, that our good behavior guarantees us a place in heaven.

Jesus Christ did not come here to find good people and attempt to make them "gooder" so they could go to heaven some day. He *"rescued us from the dominion of darkness and brought us into the kingdom"* *(Col.*

1:13). He came to take away our deadness and alienation from God and give us the power and privilege of becoming a child of God.

Before you were saved, Satan owned you. If you have experienced the new birth (John 3:3), then God owns you now. That's why it's called the new birth—you have a new Father. You start all over again (see Acts 26:18). Everyone walking around today belongs either to God or to Satan, the father of lies.

In 1 John 3:8 the Bible clearly states that Jesus came to *"destroy the devil's work"*—yet in Eph. 6:12, Paul writes that our greatest enemy is the powers of darkness. If Christ came to destroy the devil's work, why do we still have so many struggles? Despite all that they do to cause misery to others, people aren't the true villains. Principalities, powers and wicked forces are. The people who have brought the most evil and heartache your way were probably spurred on by a spirit not too far away.

I believe that every one of us, no matter what sort of family we were born into, has been set up by these demons over the years. With malicious forethought, the enemy has brought people and situations into your path to get you to scoff at God, to harden your heart so you would not believe that He loves you—or to cause you to do things that would bring such shame that you could not believe that He would forgive you.

Allowing Jesus to fix us starts with the realization that the powers of darkness don't want us fixed. After all, they're the ones that got us in the condition we're in. And they'll fight us tooth and nail as we seek our healing.

Three

When Time Doesn't Heal

"I have heard your prayer and seen your tears;
I will heal you."
—2 Kings 20:5

It's said that time heals all wounds, but in many cases this isn't true. Yes, time can ease the impact of the pain resulting from trauma and grief, but it takes a supernatural touch from the Holy Spirit to complete the work of healing. No matter how misery comes into your life, whether your own actions backfire, life throws you a curve or the heartache is demonically inspired, you will respond in the natural unless you allow the fruit of the Spirit to override your emotions. This is a choice; it takes time to learn and will never be completely automatic.

Genuine grief—especially that resulting from a lost love—can traumatize your spirit, your inner man. This provokes loneliness, resentment and anger, followed closely by guilt, disillusionment and unbelief. The logical result is incredible shame; the end result is

,thats me

withdrawal from people and God, usually in that order. If you're disillusioned with the church or with Christians, which can easily happen, you'd better watch out. Likewise if you lack faith in God. The powers of darkness will bring people into your life and set up situations that will widen that gap so much that you will end up hardening your heart to God. The spirits want you to lose hope, and they want you mad at someone somewhere, even if means making you mad at someone you love.

When I was a new Christian, God gave me an image and a scripture that He wanted me to apply to my life personally. In this image, Jesus was hanging on the cross with His arms stretched out and said, *"Father, forgive them for they know not what they do."(Lk. 23:34).* The Holy Spirit wanted me to apply Jesus' words and attitude to the people who had wounded me.

important

Some of the people who have hurt you knew exactly what they were doing, and they had no regard for the devastation their actions would cause in your life. Whether they knew it or not, their sin altered your potential for healthy relationships in the future. Unless you are healed by the Holy Spirit, that potential will be forever altered.

Yes it will

The most lasting trauma of my early years was a physical one that occurred at age five, when I broke my nose. As I grew older, it became obvious that my nose was permanently crooked. Now I had an attribute that other kids could poke fun at. And they did, relentlessly: "Crooked nose! Hump nose! Witch face!" Years later, I would hear, "Hey, tin grin! Railroad mouth," after an orthodontist decided I needed braces.

16

People who have been hurt will end up hurting others. People who don't like themselves—usually because of things that have been said or done to them—won't let you love them. Fear of even more rejection causes them to resist you and your attempts to reach out to them. You can always identify people who have been hurt. When you try to hug them, they don't hug back. The arms hang limply at their sides. How many spouses cry out for affection simply because their mate had no idea know how to return the affection they were offered? Many people grew up without expressions of love and don't know how to show the love they may genuinely feel.

I set out to find a husband, someone who would love me unconditionally as my father had. As I soon found out, dating wasn't all it was cracked up to be, especially in the "free love" days of the 1970's. Everything my mother had told me about proper behavior went right out the window, and of course, I didn't know that sexual activity outside of marriage was forbidden by the Bible. In an effort to be popular, many girls like me did things that went against their conscience, and it seared their conscience each time. We allowed ourselves to be used emotionally and physically too many times, and we were left shattered. With each rejection, we learned to hold our emotions back. With each new relationship, our prospects for genuine love are diminished.

I think I can safely say I know a little bit about trauma. I contacted one of Mick Jagger's pilots, whom I had met sometime before, and he bought me a plane ticket to Los Angeles, where one of my sisters lived. But even though I had escaped one imprisonment, I created a whole new one for myself; I spent most of my time drunk or passed out on my sister's couch.

17

I lasted five years in Hollywood and experienced enough rejection there to last a lifetime. It was a foolish decision to go there in the first place. For me, trying to fit into the Hollywood scene was as awkward as trying to take a nap in a conch shell, some things just don't fit.

Still, I kept trying. Most people thought I was aloof, proud or just not interested in them. The truth was that I had withdrawn so far inside myself that I didn't care about anything, especially meeting new people.

One night I attended the opening of a nightclub in Beverly Hills with Roberto, a date arranged by my hairdresser. I didn't know him, but he was a well-respected businessman who was handsome and wealthy, as evidenced by his Rolls Royce. Sometime early in the evening he put a knockout pill in my drink. The last thing I remember was dancing our third dance. He never called me again, and six weeks later I found myself pregnant with his child. I blamed God. Why does all this evil keep happening to me? What have I done to deserve such horrible things?

I stole some money from a friend and went to a clinic to get rid of my problem. I didn't consider the baby to be a human being; it was just another evil that had been conceived in my life. But even as I made my way home that day, I felt a loss. A part of me had died too. For a while, most days I never even got out of bed.

Could life get any worse? Well, yes, it could, as I soon found out.

One day I left a friend's house and started to hitchhike back to my own place. I didn't have any idea that was how hookers got their clients, and I was picked up by the police on a prostitution charge. It was a holiday weekend, so I was stuck in jail for five days. When I finally went to court, I was offered time served if I would plead guilty. I did.

Even with all I had been through, the powers of darkness soon came up with yet another scheme to break me. This one lasted for years and was engineered to bring me to a point of despair. It was so insidious that it nearly led me to take my own life.

Four

Freedom from Deception

"Satan himself masquerades as an angel of light."
—2 Cor. 11:14

At a time when I was the most lonely and bewildered, trying to find my purpose in life, I found myself caught in a well laid-out deception sent straight from hell.

On the way home after a very peculiar day at work, I picked up a religious pamphlet from a woman on the street. I believed there was a God, but I had no intention of getting involved with church. So I got my spiritual nourishment where I could, even if it was on a street corner.

I entered my hotel room, kicked the door shut and began to walk to my desk when I heard my name being called from behind me. Even as I turned, I knew there was no one there; the voice had come from too high above me. I looked at the ceiling, right where the sound had come from. The voice spoke again: "Chris, I'm God and I have a message for you. Don't be afraid. Your father is with me in heaven." I was awed; God was talking to me.

It wasn't God, but I didn't know it. Suddenly, for probably the first time, I felt unique. All the grief and rejection seemed to disappear as a feeling of worth washed over me.

I sat on my bed, sensing a strange power in the room. As a bright, crackling light entered my head, I felt this force enter me. I wasn't scared; after all, I thought it was God.

As the voice spoke, I wrote what it said. I was convinced I was writing the new Bible, but as I tried to convince others of the same thing, I found even more rejection and alienation. Of course, the fact that I continued living in a world of sex, drugs and rock 'n' roll was proof of the contradiction in my life, I now had an identity, a vision and a purpose. I loved communicating with the voice and seeing its predictions come true.

One day, the voice left. Devastated, I withdrew into a daily abuse of drugs. After more trouble with the law in Los Angeles, I moved to Hawaii. I realize now that through that move, the real God was calling me.

I wanted a new life in Hawaii. I knew I had to leave my destructive and ungodly relationships behind, but like many others who are searching for God, I found it impossible to develop a social life in the church. The Holy Spirit was drawing me to Christ, wanting to give me a new family, and I really tried to fit in at church, it was like my "conch shell" experience in Hollywood— some places just don't make room for you.

One Sunday I had a particularly crushing experience. The worship leader, who looked so pure that she made me long for my lost innocence, approached me after church and asked if I knew God. "Of course I do," I answered. "I'm writing the new Bible. God came to my hotel and explained it all to me." She quickly left me and rejoined her friends. It didn't take long for her to tell everyone that I was nuts.

For the next nine months, I attended church alone, at times hung over. It seemed I didn't fit anywhere, and now even the voice wouldn't talk to me. The alienation I felt was authentic; the demons had me right where they wanted me. Suicide seemed the best answer. After all, the voice had told me that we all come back to life, so I figured I should start over.

But the prayers of a righteous person are powerful and effective (James 5:16), and my Baptist grandmother had spent a great deal of time on her knees for me. Finally, one day her efforts paid off.

A man from church asked if he could see the new Bible I was writing. I was thrilled that he was taking me seriously. What I didn't realize was that he was well aware that the supernatural events in my life were not from God. He began to pray before he opened my stack of notebooks.

As he prayed, a myriad of thoughts flooded my mind: memories of all the years I'd spent trying to do something for the voice inside, all the loneliness and frustration, two stints in mental wards, all trying to prove God had come to me. My life was in a shambles.

Suddenly, truth overwhelmed me.

"God didn't do this, did He?" I asked.

My life was a lie, and I knew it. I became indignant and angry. Why did God let me think I knew Him all these years when I didn't? Why did He let me think I was His special agent and must write the new Bible? My anger turned to shock, because in that moment all my dreams and purpose disappeared. I was desolate and naked, and my soul was at stake.

"Chris, your lifestyle gave Satan the right to deceive you," my friend said. "Now God has shown you the truth. It's up to you now to decide who you want to follow."

I decided for God.

At my friend's suggestion, I became involved with Youth With A Mission, even though at twenty-nine I felt I was too old for any group that had "youth" in its name. But YWAM was based in Hawaii at the time, and it seemed like as good a place to start as any. It took me several months of trying to live like a Christian on my own before I gave in and enrolled in YWAM's missionary training program.

During my second day in the program, the demon left me—with a horrible, audible groan. Jesus was now my whole life. That day, when God replaced my heart of stone with a new, soft heart, a supernatural battle began. The powers of hell did all they could to get me to revert to old patterns of thinking. Anger, hatred, rebellion, fear of rejection, bitterness and a multitude of other sins were just waiting in the wings to manipulate me. With a new, soft heart, I was more vulnerable than ever.

But the Father, through His Son, had wonderful plans for me, plans for things that never would have entered my mind. He gave me a family of mission workers and a vision for doing work in His kingdom, for a while, life was great. I could now love and be loved. Years of hurt melted away as the Holy Spirit renewed my mind.

Five

Peace through Forgiveness

"See to it that no one misses the grace of God."
—Heb. 12:15

If we could learn to call upon the supernatural grace that God offers instead of reacting according to the sin nature inside us, then our hearts would stay soft. But we need also to learn not to stuff offenses down inside of us. If we continue to do that, before long we'll have more grudges piled up than we can handle, and we're likely to explode in anger. As you learn to depend on God's grace in time of need, you'll discover an unexplainable peace.

One time on the mission field one of the girls in my charge did something purely by accident that offended the Hindu principal of the school where we were ministering. The longer I remained calm as he viciously confronted me, the angrier he got. He wanted a reaction, but God's grace enabled me to keep my composure. That's the kind of peace I'm talking about.

I want this kind of peace.

27

Although Moses did a number of things that could have brought him disfavor with God, it seems that it was his temper that eventually cost him the promised land (Num. 20:12). God had told Moses to speak to a rock and it would bring forth water. Moses became angry with the Israelites and struck the rock instead. When he did, he misrepresented God's character—which is slow to anger. When we bite the bullet instead of calling on the grace of God, we will eventually blow our top too.

Besides defiling those around us with our bitterness, our anger can literally make us sick. I read about a man in Australia who had an operation that left a small hole in his stomach. With his permission, the doctors ran a series of tests to gauge the physical repercussions of the conversations the man had. When the man spoke about something in his life that irritated him, his body secreted a poisonous chemical. Through this study and others doctors have concluded that prolonged anger can result in all sorts of physical disorders.

If you carry around an offense or try to bury your anger instead of dealing with it, you may end up physically sick. The Word of God admonishes us to "cast all [our] anxiety on him because he cares for [us]" (1 Pet. 5:7). He cares enough to keep us from doing things that would damage our bodies.

Over the years I've preached to thousands of people, but I've never forgotten one woman who responded to an altar call I gave. The call was specifically for those who wanted to repent of unforgiveness in their lives. The elderly woman was bent over, and anguish and bitterness were etched deeply in her face. I asked her why she had come to the altar. With a raspy voice she said, "I hate my husband."

A few heads turned, and I signaled to the worship team to play louder. I didn't want anyone else to hear this, especially her husband. "How long have you hated your husband?" I asked. "Nine years," she said. I told her to ask God out loud to forgive her for anything in her heart that shouldn't be there, starting with unforgiveness.

As I began to pray for her, she immediately fell to the floor. No one caught her. She didn't land with a particularly loud thud, so I assumed she was OK and moved on to the next person in line. After praying for several more people, I looked back at her and hardly recognized her. She was standing straight, and years of wrinkles were gone from her face. She didn't look the same at all. No matter what psychiatrists say about the benefits of "healthy anger," God tells us not to hold on to it: *"Do not let the sun go down while you are still angry, and do not give the devil a foothold"* (Eph. 4:26-27). As soon as this woman gave up her anger, she was transformed. The devil no longer had a foothold in her life.

REMINDER

I'm convinced that the powers of darkness work overtime at finding something or someone that will be a continual thorn in your life, some situation that's out of your control. Even if it takes years to set you up, Satan is constantly on the prowl to devour you.

Whatever—or whoever—you're stuck with now, the thing or person that irritates you the most is the very thing you must give to Jesus. Let Him fill you with supernatural grace to endure! Peter writes, *" . . . Christ suffered for you, leaving you an example, that you should follow in his steps" (1 Pet. 2:21).* Jesus didn't sin, didn't lie and didn't answer back when He was insulted. He left His case in the hands of the one who judges fairly.

How does the enemy get a foothold? Our unforgiveness gives him an entrance. You see, we all have something precious and valuable in us—our spirit man. It's who we are, and it's going to live forever. As blows come to our spirit, it's natural that our heart and emotions are affected. The Bible says, *"Guard your heart, for it is the wellspring of life" (Prov. 4:23).* Why? Because Satan can put things in our heart that will bring to the surface the sin that's already there. Satan put it in the heart of Judas to betray Jesus and into the heart of Ananias to lie to Peter.

The enemy sends the catalyst for heartache, gets us to respond and then jumps on the bandwagon, magnifying the wrongs and fueling our anger until we sin. Don't get me wrong—we are responsible for our own sin. But through attacks from demons, through their whispers or their manipulation of people around us, we can end up living in the flesh and responding in the natural. Jesus said, *". . . The prince of this world is coming. He has no hold on me" (John 14:30).* Can you say that today, or does the enemy have a hold on you? Has he been successful in planting resentment, bitterness and unbelief in your heart?

If you feel that the enemy has a foothold on your emotions, thoughts or attitudes, then why not loosen that grip? Yes, you probably have every right to be angry about some of the things that have been done to you, but the spiritual repercussions are simply not worth it. You can't move forward with God until you get your heart and conscience clean.

Remember this, though: It's one thing to ask God to help you to forgive, but that's not repentance. You'll discover that release and peace come much more quickly and easily if you tell God that you are choosing to forgive. Asking God to take away the hatred you harbor for another person doesn't cut it either. Isaiah confessed, *". . . I am a man of unclean lips . . ." (Isa. 6:5)*. He didn't say, Lord, take this uncleanness away. Do you see the difference? What God takes away when you genuinely repent is the hurt, the shame, the guilt, the fear. We are held responsible to stop the sin we embrace due to hurts.

Years ago, I read about an experiment conducted on rats to see if they could survive with human blood in their bodies. They lived about twenty-four minutes. But when one rat was given blood from a man who had just exploded in anger, the rat died within seconds. Now I have no way of confirming that this actually happened, but I know what the Bible has to say about wrath. You can read for yourself in Scripture how concerned God is about the way we respond and cling to the assaults that come into our lives.

When we recite the Lord's prayer, we forget what comes after the "amen": *"For if you forgive men when they sin against you, your heavenly Father will also forgive you. But if you do not forgive men their sins, your Father will not forgive your sins" (Matt. 6:14-15)*.

A mere four chapters later, Jesus gives us fair warning about those nearest to us: *"A man's enemies will be the members of his own household" (Matt. 10:36)*. Relatives will probably reject you, ostracize you or just plain bug you the most. You can bet the powers of darkness will instigate and manipulate arguments with your relatives in order to get you to stay away from your family. Satan wants you hurt and offended so you will stop witnessing to them. I've walked on eggshells around members of my family—or even avoided them—simply because I knew they would pick a fight. *same*

After years of prayer and witnessing to certain loved ones, I found that I had given up and had hardened my heart to them. That way, if they died without Christ, I might be able to stand the pain. It's traumatic enough when a loved one dies, but it's even harder to bear if you know they purposely rejected Christ. As my mother moved up in age, I found myself looking for things that would help me "unlove" my mother. I was certain she would die—unsaved—while I was serving overseas with YWAM, and the pain would be too great for me to bear. Fortunately, one day she kneeled by her bed and asked Christ into her heart, proving that you should never give up fighting for your family.

Jesus says to *"let your light shine before men, that they may see your good deeds and praise your Father in heaven" (Matt. 5:16).* But what if people see your good deeds and don't seem to care? First of all, we don't know what God is doing in another person's heart, no matter how they may respond to us. At a low point in my life, God prompted me to send a book to my aunt. I knew she was sick, but I was not in a hurry to write yet another letter to her. I figured she'd ignore it as she had all the others I'd sent, so I procrastinated. Weeks later, I wrote her a letter that told about all the neat things God had done that year and included it in a package with the book. When I called my grandmother to get my aunt's zip code, I found out Aunt Dottie had died that morning.

We can never tell about God's goodness often enough, so don't let fear of rejection keep you from proclaiming His goodness. Remember, *"You are a chosen people, a royal priesthood, a holy nation, a people belonging to God, that you may declare the praises of him who called you out of darkness into his wonderful light" (1 Pet. 2:9).*

Six

Never Give Up

*"I pray also that the eyes of your heart may be
enlightened in order that you may know the hope
to which he has called you."*
—Eph. 1:18

Anyone who's ever been on a short-term missions
trip understands what it's like to minister without the
benefit of seeing the fruit of their work. When I was
with YWAM, I couldn't always stay in one place long
enough to see my efforts through. On the other hand,
mobility had its advantages; I also didn't have to endure
the scorn of people who didn't appreciate my
witnessing.

When I returned to the U.S., I faced a problem
that many of you have encountered: how to handle daily
rejection of your witness, especially in the workplace.
Through God's leading, I ended up in Minneapolis,
where I knew no one and where I had to start from

scratch introducing my ministry to churches where I hoped to speak. As I began scheduling preaching engagements, I took a part-time job telemarketing janitorial cleaning services. That was a bummer in itself. I mean, what on earth did this have to do with being a preacher?

One morning I met a man named Jim who was waiting to be interviewed for a position that would make him my boss. I prayed that he would get the job and even told him so when he returned for a second interview. Being a missionary overseas had ignited in me a freedom to talk to anyone about God. I wasn't going to stop just because I was back in the states—or so I thought.

Jim got the job, and suddenly I became concerned that he was going to scrutinize me because I had been so bold about my faith. I needn't have worried, though. He treated me kindly from the start. What I should have worried about was the way I was scrutinizing him.

I was awestruck by him, and I felt like a young schoolgirl. He was so handsome. Every female feeling I had buried so long came screaming to the surface. Almost immediately, I thought, Now I know why God brought me to Minneapolis—He's going to save Jim and give him to me!

Those of you who have been in the same predicament are having a good laugh right now. I assume I'm not the first person who became attracted to someone I was supposed to be leading to the Lord.

Jim, who was Catholic, made sure each Monday that I knew he had attended Mass over the weekend. He had a heart for God, but his lifestyle showed no evidence of the new birth. I asked God to zap him and accelerate his spiritual growth so he could catch up with me and help me in ministry. God had an answer, and it wasn't the one I wanted to hear. He let me know that Jim was not the man for me but that I would have spiritual input into his life.

After many disappointing times when Jim had declined my invitations to attend Christian events with me, finally he agreed to come hear me preach. I wanted to convince him that God had a ministry for him, too—hopefully, with me. Even though a friend warned me that I was totally out of order and my emotions were going to get me in hot water with God, I decided that Jim could help me pray for people who responded to the altar call. Normally, there are not enough workers for the number of people who respond.

On the way to the church, I instructed Jim about what to do: "All you need to do, Jim, is ask God to show them what's in their heart that they need to repent of, and then have them pray a prayer of repentance," I said. "Then take the oil and put it on their forehead and say whatever comes to mind while you pray for them."

During the altar call close to eighty people lined up across the front. I called for the church prayer counselors, but I was told they were in the line themselves; a half hour before the service, the church board had resigned and this was to be the pastor's last service as well. Eagerly I handed Jim the bottle of oil and said, "You're on." I had to remind him what to do. He started out by simply placing oil on the foreheads of one person after another without praying with them. Twice I saw Jim crying as he prayed, something I do often as people share their pain. I just knew he was perfect for altar work and perfect for me.

A few months later, without seeking God, I went to work for a competitor. Jim was in no hurry to move forward with God, and I simply couldn't be around him anymore. When I told him I was leaving, he said, "I love you, Chris, but I'm not attracted to you." As major rejection hit, I became my usual blunt self. I looked him squarely in the face and said, "If you're the one God has for me and you blow it, I'll never forgive you."

Not only had Jim rejected me, but he hadn't gotten saved either. What had been the point? I wondered. Leery that I was outside of God's will because I hadn't prayed about the job change, I nonetheless settled into my new office. Much to my surprise, Jim took a job there as well several weeks later. I figured God was giving me more time to lead him to Christ—or maybe to me!

But now Jim treated me differently. My feelings for him were out in the open, and now he was very aloof. Even worse, Jim was a lousy salesman and my commission was based on his sales. Once again, without praying about it, I quit and hoped I'd never see him again. Little by little my former childlike dependence on God's guidance was being changed by my own need for self-preservation.

Several months later, though, God clearly led me to "... *go back to the land of my relatives...* " *(Gen. 31:3)*— the Eastern Shore of Maryland, where my family now lived. Just before I left, Jim called and asked for a favor. It was clear that God had been dealing with him.

That day I had the privilege of leading Jim to the Lord. As he prayed, I realized that even attractive people suffer from rejection. As I ministered to him, my own desire for him changed. I loved him in a godly way now, more like a parent. I even baptized him in the icy waters of the pool at my apartment complex (spring in Minnesota is not a time to go swimming). It was a very special day.

Yes, Jim did have a calling on his life. I ended up training him to take my place as an interviewer on a Christian radio station. He stayed there for a year — and then he entered seminary!

Don't ever stop having input into people's lives. Don't let the rejection stop you from inviting people to church. Rejection from nonbelievers can hurt if you take the rejection personally, but remember that *". . . the god of this age has blinded the minds of unbelievers . . . " (2 Cor. 4:4).* It's usually not you they dislike; it's the darkness in them avoiding the light in you. So let your light shine, and expect to be surprised only when they don't reject you.

Seven

Devoured by the Church

*"Therefore, as we have opportunity, let us do good
to all people, especially to those who
belong to the family of believers."*
—*Gal. 6:10*

For many of us, the love that God shed abroad in
our heart at the new birth will be drained by those in
the church, since they are the people we are usually
closest to. Paul issued this warning to the church in
Galatia: *"If you keep on biting and devouring each
other, watch out or you will be destroyed by each other"
(Gal. 5:15).*

We don't expect those in the church to bite and
devour each other. Remember the Dalmatian tied to the
fence? Lots of us react the way he did, and as a result,
there's a chain reaction that results in someone else
being bitten.

On my first assignment to Samoa, I was to head
up a drama team—my only purpose in being there. But

by the time I arrived, a new director was in place, and he decided that I would be the hospitality girl—a fancy name for base maid. We obviously started off on the wrong foot; he simply wouldn't back down, and I had no choice but to submit.

I had to share sleeping quarters with seven rambunctious Samoans who never stopped talking. I asked the director if I could move one of the spare bunks to a quieter area, but he refused my request. Now for someone who was used to having things go her way, this submission thing was a new concept, but I complied.

Within weeks, I was desperate to get away. A huge YWAM celebration was about to be held in Hawaii, and any missionary who could afford the plane ticket could go. I was the only one from Samoa who would be going. I knew the director wanted to go, but I wasn't about to give him money to come with me. After all the times we had butted heads, I wanted a reprieve from him.

You can probably guess what happened—God started nudging me to buy his plane ticket. You must be kidding! I thought. Eventually God won, but I was still worldly enough to ask the director for a favor in return— a quiet bunk away from the seven Samoan sleep-killers. We didn't tell anyone about our trade, but when he started to show favoritism toward me the others on base began to bite and devour me with looks and gossip.

Instead of rejoicing with someone who had been blessed, these women had chosen to take the natural and fleshly route that leads to envy and resentment. They gave me the cold shoulder, and I reacted like the Dalmatian, sitting on my tail.

God taught me two lessons through this situation. One, some of the hardest-hearted people in church are those who have been hurt the most. Now they are defensive and take it out on others. Our hurts cause us to hurt others by withdrawing.

The second lesson? Give obediently and cheerfully —and don't turn your gift into an opportunity to bribe!

Eight

Costly Betrayal

"If anyone causes one of these little ones who believe in me to sin, it would be better for him to be thrown into the sea with a large millstone tied around his neck."
—Mark 9:42

Looking back on my seventeen years as a Christian, I can see places where I walked right into a setup from Satan. In the beginning I was fairly buoyant, but over time, my tail wagged a whole lot less than it did in the beginning.

One of the enemy's setups resulted in the worst and longest-standing offense I've ever had to endure. It started years ago, and it simply can't seem to be fixed. Some of you will be able to relate to it, because you too have been swindled by a brother or sister in Christ.

The whole ordeal started in 1984 when I met—and was mesmerized by—a well-known evangelist whose best-seller on personal miracles had placed him in the spotlight. The following year when I saw him again, he told me God was raising up certain men to protect the assets of those Christians who would be alive during the tribulation. Being new in the Lord, I took him at his word. That summer, I saw him again and told him I had decided to leave everything to YWAM in my will. "Everything" included an inheritance of nearly a half million dollars.

"Don't leave everything to one organization, because they may go off the rails some day," he said, offering instead to set up a trust fund for me. Under the terms, the interest would support me while I was alive, and upon my death, the principal would be released to support mission groups.

It sounded good to me, and unfortunately, those I sought counsel from were also awed by this man's reputation. We set up the trust fund, but when my inheritance came through six months later, he tied it up in a timeshare investment and claimed it as a donation to his evangelistic organization. In all, he took $480,000 from me. For several years I let him slide because of who he was. He would occasionally apologize and offer to return my money, but he never did. I once met a pastor from Los Angeles who told me three people in his congregation had also been swindled by "Rev. Doe," as I now refer to him. It seemed this highly renowned evangelist would go from one church to another seeking naive people like me.

For years I took out loans to travel to Los Angeles from the mission field in order to meet with him in the presence of Christian mediators. Each time he would repent in tears and later renege. All of this took its toll on my joy and left me in sheer bewilderment that Christians could behave this way.

Money does funny things to people. Maybe you've given money to a church for a specific purpose only to find out later that your offering was used improperly. Others of you may have been betrayed by a business partner or simply conned the way I was. What good would it do any of us to remain bitter for years? I admit that this ordeal has been frustrating, but bitterness would have only stunted my growth in God and probably given me ulcers, at the very least.

God warns us not to pay back evil for evil (Rom. 12:17); He reminds us that vengeance must be left to Him (Rom. 12:19). The Bible also tells us that *". . . false prophets [and] false teachers . . . will exploit you with deceptive words . . . " (2 Pet. 2:1,3).* Even the early church had its problems with swindlers in the flock; the first eight verse of 1 Corinthians 6 establishes the procedure believers should take when they've been cheated by another Christian.

But while Christian mediators may help settle a dispute, they're powerless to stop these wolves in sheep's clothing from continuing in a pulpit ministry. Christian conciliation services wouldn't be needed if pastors could mediate squabbles. But any honest pastor will tell you that in most cases he has very little authority over a church member and absolutely none over a visitor who arrives with his own agenda.

Humans—including Christian humans!—generally dislike authority. Yet we are commanded to *"submit . . . to every authority instituted among men . . . " (1 Pet. 2:13).* This includes those in church leadership who pilfer parishoners. They should be subjected to the law of the land. Is it valid, at times, to use the legal system as your only recourse? Some say, yes.

Once discovered, a deceitful minister can simply move to another area and begin swindling a fresh, new congregation. Who can bring these men into account before God sends them to their ultimate doom? If a Christian will not submit to the authority of the church, then the conciliation procedure described in 1 Corinthians 6 is difficult to apply. The secular court system seems to be the only option for those who disregard biblical warnings.

In my case, Christian leaders from a credible mission group tried for three years to bring Rev. Doe into account. I believed I should not sue him, so I left the case in God's hands. Surely He could change Rev. Doe's heart. In 1989 I tried a second Christian conciliation service. After three days of meetings, Doe signed an agreement to return my funds but again reneged. Even Rev. Doe's own board of directors couldn't get him to return my funds. He started sending small checks sporadically to keep me at bay and out of court.

Eventually, an attorney helped pro bono. He had enough clout to scare Rev. Doe, who offered me $200,000 in payments over several years. My lawyer said no. His actions had added up to include criminal racketeering charges under the RICO law, which we did not pursue.

Finally, in June of 1994—nearly ten years after I first met him—Doe was convicted of fraud, and a judgment of $1.1 million was awarded to me. Five years later, I have yet to see a cent of that judgment. Doe has proven that he is accountable to no one.

My main concern, though, is that Doe continues to preach, despite the judgment against him. Pastors and organizations, well aware of his fraud conviction, continue to embrace him and invite him to preach.

Forgiving Doe hasn't been an issue for me; I did that long ago. But there have been repercussions, especially among my loved ones. In some cases, the damage has so far been irreparable; others in my family, though, have witnessed the way God in His mercy and faithfulness has provided for me financially. Even though God forgives, He also disciplines, and I have to believe that someday God will call Doe to account for his inappropriate behavior.

No matter what anyone has done to hurt you, look past the offense to the way Satan set you up. Satan wants you to doubt God's love and scoff at His sovereignty. Paul warns us that there will be those in the church that Satan has sent for just that purpose.

If we allow God to heal our hurts and soften our heart through our repentance and His supernatural touch, then we will be less apt to judge other believers. We have no idea what experiences have made others vulnerable to the demons that manipulate them. "Don't let your anger lead you into scoffing at God—and don't allow your suffering to embitter you against the only one who can deliver you." (Job 35:18, *Living Bible*, Tyndale House, 1971)

HOPE

Nine

When Hope Is Gone

*"Do not throw away your confidence; it will be
richly rewarded. You need to persevere so that when
you have done the will of God, you will
receive what he has promised."*
—Heb. 10:35-36

Most Christians say they love God. But how much
does that love fluctuate? Do you love Him as much as
you did when you first believed? Is your love as strong
as it was a few years ago, last month or even yesterday?

Does your love change along with your faith? Paul
suggests in 2 Cor. 10:15 that our faith grows. Likewise,
there are times when it's at a standstill or even
regressing. What does that do to our love for God?

It's entirely possible to be stymied in the faith
department as we wait to see God come through for
us. But our faith becomes strong and steady during those
times when we've seen God deliver us out of our
troubles, making the wait worthwhile after all.

Our memories of what God has done for us should bring us to a deeper level of faith. But when it comes to lost hope—or a lost heart—our memories can have a negative effect on our faith. After all, how can you have faith if your hope is gone? Those things that have gone wrong can easily overshadow all that has gone right. Notice in Matt. 16:8-9 how Jesus rebukes the disciples: *"You of little faith, why are you talking among yourselves about having no bread? . . . Don't you remember the five loaves for the five thousand, and how many basketfuls you gathered?"* The disciples themselves had trouble remembering the miracles they had witnessed with their own eyes.

After a number of years in the pulpit, I looked back with concern at the hundreds of people who had stood at the altar, torn by grief over the hurts they had endured. They had no joy, vision or hope for a better future. I had always bounced back; why couldn't they? The answer was just around the corner.

By the time God moved me "to the land of my relatives," I was weary from all it took to be an itinerant evangelist—the endless hours on the phone trying to book speaking engagements and the extreme loneliness, among other things. I had no friends other than people I had ministered to in the Midwest and overseas, and now I had to start over once again in a strange town.

I found a small, quaint cottage on the Chesapeake Bay on the Eastern Shore of Maryland and started to settle in. I began attending meetings of the local ministerium in order to make myself known and was eventually elected vice president. That opened a lot of doors for me, and I became involved with food banks, tutoring and working with kids in nearby housing projects. My family was also nearby, and I was grateful to show them in person how much God had changed me. For a while life was good.

After ten months—just when I was beginning to develop something of a social life—God moved me to Virginia Beach. This was right at the time when the useless judgment against Rev. Doe came about, and I was feeling at bay with God. After all these years, why hadn't He come through?

The Bible says God tests us that we may see what is in our own heart. Even with all my memories of the times God had come through for me, I was about to be sent into the worst tailspin of my Christian life. In some circles, I would have been branded a backslider.

You've probably heard that people tend to forget God during the good times and draw closer to Him during the bad times. At times, the opposite has been true for me. When all is well, I enjoy lounging around with Him for hours, reading the Bible or other books. When I moved to Virginia Beach, I found myself thinking about some of the specific unanswered prayers in my life. God appeared to be silent, and confusion set in. I sulked and withdrew from Him. As doubt and hopelessness took root, my desire to pray waned and I headed toward spiritual numbness.

Once again, I was the new kid in town, and I was tired of trying to meet new people. It didn't matter how many times I stood in a new church introducing myself as a new neighbor, no one really cared. Their lives were too busy already to make room for yet another relationship. My faith was crumbling. As my hope for a bright—and wealthy—future disappeared, I racked my brain trying to figure out what I had done to deserve the situation I was in. I didn't ask God about it, because I was afraid of His silence. Giving up seemed to be the answer. I felt God had rejected me by not giving me my money back and, for that matter, by not giving me a husband!

This is precisely the deception the serpent used on Eve in the garden—that God was withholding something from her. Once we begin to mistrust God's character, disobedience has easy access. I wondered why God wouldn't "... *rouse Himself on my behalf...*" *(see Job 8:6, NAS)* as He had promised over the years. If He wasn't going to do what He said, then why believe? If God isn't for me, then who is?

When children don't get what they want, they show their true colors. They say mean things to their parents. Few of us would openly say mean things to God, so instead we withdraw and live with false assumptions. If God hasn't answered my prayer—which must be a good prayer, since I want it answered—then I assume that He has in a way rejected me.

Moving to Virginia Beach had come about suddenly, and although God had confirmed this move through scripture, I felt uneasy. I was now in my forties and flabbergasted that no potential mate had crossed my path, despite all the churches I'd been in. If God had someone for me on the horizon, I'd better make sure I was in the right town.

Shortly after my move, I was crying in bed one night and spoke aloud to the Lord. "God, I want to remind You that I'm single, and if You keep moving me, how am I ever going to find a mate?" I asked. "Please, will You do something that proves to me I'm in the center of your will here—something that can't possibly be a coincidence?" Before I even finished praying, I said out loud that I wanted to speak to Pat Robertson.

I sat there stunned. Now why did I say that? I had met Robertson briefly years before when Sheila Welsh interviewed me on *The 700 Club*, but the chances of talking to him face-to-face were slim at best. When my first book was released in America, I had tried unsuccessfully to get back on the show. What chance did I have now—unless I spoke directly to Pat Robertson himself?

The next day I felt the urge to get out of my apartment and wandered over to a nearby mall. I really felt alone, sitting there watching other people go by. A man asked if he and his wife could sit next to me. I glanced over to give a cordial smile and see if I should do some witnessing, when I found myself face-to-face with—you guessed it, Pat Robertson.

Needless to say, he didn't need my witnessing. We started talking, and he graciously waited while I retrieved a copy of my book from my car. We chatted for a while about the possibility of me appearing on *The 700 Club* again, and as I drove home I found myself once again in awe of God's sovereignty. To place Pat Robertson right next to me within a day of that request was incredible. It proved again what a loving and faithful Father we have, one who is eager to encourage us knowing that sometimes we get weary and our vision gets blurred.

In the opening verse of Psalm 43:1-2, David prays, *"Vindicate me, O God, and plead my cause against an ungodly nation; rescue me from deceitful and wicked men."* This was his prayer that day, and it was as important as anything you might have prayed today.

TRUST

He goes on to say, *"You are God my stronghold."* In other words, God, this is what I want You to do, and You're the only one who can do it. But then he asks some strange questions in the midst of his request and his affirmation of God's power: *"Why have you rejected me? Why must I go about mourning, oppressed by the enemy?" (Verse 2).* As we wait to see God affirm His love and nearness through answered prayer, too many of us allow an old tape to start playing in our heads. It's an old message that reminds us of all those who have hurt us, of all the doors that never opened and the dreams that were blocked by other people.

Vivid pictures of the evil they did linger in our minds, and any decent doctor will tell you that harboring such images can result in introversion to the point of paranoia. But even as despondent as David was, another tape started playing in his head, one that served as a to counterattack to the rejection he was feeling. He remembers God's track record. David chews out his soul for being downcast and makes the decision to praise God.

Many react the way I did when God was quiet. We search ourselves to see if He is punishing us, and often we take God's silence—or His "No"—as a personal rejection. The memories of shattered dreams rise to the surface, leaving us numb to any stirrings of hope within us.

The Old Testament describes numerous accounts of godly men who built altars as a sign that God had revealed Himself to them. They did this to signify that God had spoken a command, given them a promise of a future event, brought an encouraging word or simply issued a directive. Noah built an altar as soon as he left the ark. Abraham built one in remembrance of God's promise to him that God would give the land to his offspring. Jacob built an altar when God promised to return him to his own household.

As time went by, life got tough and God appeared to be silent, these men remembered the altars they had built. No matter what doubts came or how many obstacles stood in their way, they had the altar as a tangible object to remind them of God's promises. They didn't need to stop and scratch their heads and wonder, "Did God really speak to me?" They didn't question whether God was going to keep His promise. They remembered building that altar and the joy they experienced as they gathered stones to build it. The altar gave them a reason to continue, to be filled with hope and to claim their future victory.

Ten

Erasing Old Tapes

"Find rest, O my soul, in God alone;
my hope comes from him."
—*Psalm 62:5*

I once knew a girl named Ann. We met on a small private island in the Chesapeake Bay, where my family spent weekends and most summers all through my teenage years. Ann and I competed at tennis, swimming and sailing, and crossed paths at night when we sneaked out of our houses. We attended the same parties, but Ann never talked to me. She was the pretty one, and I was not.

One night after I became a Christian, I had a dream about Ann. We were at a reunion, and everyone was talking and laughing but us. We had nothing to say, no memories to recall. As I looked at her across the table, she suddenly stood up, looked me in the eye and said, "I never let you know me, did I?"

The dream was so vivid that I woke up with tears in my eyes. I realized Ann represented all the attractive, "together" people I had wanted to get to know over the years. They were the ones who looked like Barbie dolls, while I resembled Lucy from the Peanuts comic strip.

When people have rejected you, you can develop an ungodly behavior pattern. Any time I saw a person who was vivacious, stunning and confident, I assumed they wouldn't want to know me, and I headed in the opposite direction. Of course, as I made a u-turn, I judged the person for being proud or snobbish. I forfeited potential friendships because I assumed I would be rejected.

The fear of rejection can also cause a dream to die. As a child, I wanted to become an ice dancer like those I saw at the Ice Capades. At night, I would fall asleep visualizing myself being twirled around by some strong, handsome boy. Each Saturday, I would put on my little outfit, go to the skating rink and wait expectantly as the "couples only" song was played. The boys lined up on one side, the girls on the other. I would keep hoping someone would pick me, but no one ever did. Then the lights would come back on—along with the humiliation of being one of the dorky girls left standing alone by the rails.

Eventually, when it came time for "couples only," I went to the snack bar or pretended I had to re-tie my laces. Ultimately, I gave up the dream and didn't go back. I don't care anymore. Why bother? I give up.

Another dream of mine was to become a cheerleader. I tried out every year but I was always one of the first to be cut. In my senior year, my mother asked me if I was going to try out again. By then, I was numb. I don't care anymore. Why bother? I give up.

My parents thought I was on drugs even before I was. I had no interest in getting involved in anything. I had given up. As my hopes were dashed over and over again, I developed a built-in defense that enabled me to harden my heart.

When we feel hopeless, that old familiar "I give up" tape clicks on—even for believers. Countless Christians who are supposed to be running the race with endurance are instead crawling the race hoping they just cross the finish line. They may hold their breath, cross their fingers or just make it by the skin of their teeth— it doesn't matter how, as long as they get in. They want to love God, but their hearts have moved from Him and they find themselves *". . . running aimlessly . . . like a man beating the air" (1 Cor. 9:26).*

When we give up and abandon our trust in God, our worship soon becomes dry and God seems even farther away. This attitude seeps into our Christian walk unannounced and swallows up our faith. Instead of praying "God, let Your will be done," we instead say in defeat "Do whatever—You're going to do that anyway." Sometimes we may even find ourselves expecting Him to be so vengeful that He will do the opposite of our heart's desire.

That's why it's so important for us to never forget our spiritual altars or the words God has given us regarding specific situations. Then, when God is quiet, we're less apt to give up or jump the gun, because we've learned to wait on Him. By thinking back to a time when the heavens opened and the spirit of God revealed a promise, a direction and an answer to our heart's request, we have hope for our present and future circumstances.

Psalm 130:5 states, *"I wait for the LORD, my soul waits, and in his word I put my hope."* The "word" in this verse refers to the spoken word of God rather than the written Word, the Bible. Many a Christian has seen their faith shipwrecked because they were waiting for God to do something He never told them He would do. The men who made altars and waited in hope for God to do something already had a "word" from Him. Likewise, the women: in Luke 1:45, Elizabeth says to Mary, *"Blessed is she who has believed that what the Lord has said to her will be accomplished!"* That promise was a spoken word from God.

God has never failed to give me a word if I diligently sought him, but too often I grew impatient or didn't like what I heard and fought it. I quit waiting on the Lord and did what I thought was best. I wonder how many blessings I may have missed by not seeking the Lord. I ignored the truth that He will do what He says He will do. It's up to me to wait for that still, small voice revealing His will for me. *"Are God's consolations not enough for you, words spoken gently to you?"* (Job 15:11).

The day that we ask Jesus to come into our lives, our hearts are overjoyed and filled with excitement. The words "Your will be done" come easily, and we say them with great hope and conviction. Then the trials and adversity come. Those words that once were so easily spoken lose their zest. The numbness sneaks in and all hope is deferred. Waiting for results has made our heart sick. But Scripture states, *"You will keep in perfect peace him whose mind is steadfast, because he trusts in you"* (Isa. 26:3). Ahh . . . so this is the secret. Our peace comes from keeping our mind on Him. But is our mind set on Him because we trust in God's perfect timing and plan for our lives—or is our mind set on

TRUST

Him because we trust Him to do what we want Him to do? If we trust Him hard enough, will that move His hand?

Scripture declares over and over again that God is all-powerful, faithful and abounding in lovingkindness. His mercy is new every morning. His Word promises that all things will work together for good for those who love Him, that He does not withhold any good thing and that He will grant the desires of our hearts.

Knowing—and believing—what the Bible says should fill me with great hope, but unfortunately my memory banks are also filled with situations that didn't work out the way I had hoped they would. At times, it seemed as though God had chosen not to give me the desire of my heart. I am still waiting for certain desires to be fulfilled. Like many saints, I find myself wondering, Will God help me, or should I go ahead and just do what seems best?

Scripture tells us that if we believe, we will see great things occur. My experience would tell me something different if I allowed it to. At one time early on in my Christian walk, God answered a resounding no to three of my prayer requests. I felt that maybe the best was over and, just like other relationships that had started out with a bang, this one with God had fizzled out too. My old rejection tape clicked on, and I got a bit rude as I talked to God one night.

As I looked through my Bible, though, several verses from Job leaped out at me: *"Why has your heart carried you away, and why do your eyes flash, so that you vent your rage against God and pour out such words from your mouth?" (Job 15:12-13).* Then I flipped the pages back to Job 9:12 and read this: *"Who can say to him, 'What are you doing?'"* I decided it was time for me to read Job again.

I came away from my reading that night with the understanding that God does say no. The answer He had given me wasn't even a "No, not now"—it was a "No, it can never be!" I also understood that God was not treating me unjustly, but that He knows the whole picture while I see only what is in front of me. Sometimes I have had to wait years to find out why I got a no answer from God. My trust and hope in God comes from all the times I have seen Him come through. Like David, I need to remember God's track record and I must choose to hope again in Him.

Think of all the times God has come through. Look at all He has done for you. That's where your trust comes in. That is why making memories with Him are so important. He said He would do something, and He did it. Use those memories as your altar, and claim the word that the Holy Spirit has given you while you wait for God's will.

Unfortunately, though, some of us have the same nature as Job's comforters. We rack our brains to find out why God isn't doing what we expected Him to. Not only do we fear a "no" answer, but also we expect the worst from the one we should trust the most. Because people have let us down, subconsciously we figure, God will do the same.

I call this the squished bird syndrome. The year I lived by the Chesapeake Bay, I notice piles of broken and empty clamshells strewn across the road. Each day newer ones would appear near the old dried ones. I eventually realized that one lone sea gull was the culprit. He would bring the clams back from the bay one by one and drop them from about twenty feet in the air so they would break on impact. Then he'd land and pick out his lunch. I thought he was pretty clever.

One morning as I watched two finches eating from the bird feeder outside my window, I thought of Jesus' words in Matt. 6:26 — *"Look at the birds of the air; they do not sow or reap or store away in barns, and yet your heavenly Father feeds them . . . "* Yes, He does. Have you ever seen a bird dive beak-first into the ground to retrieve a worm? How did he know it was there? But on this morning I took some credit for the finches' nourishment; after all they were eating because I spent $1.69 at the market to get seed, so God fed them through me. As long as they didn't mind my big black cat staring at them through the window, they got an easy meal.

Later that day, I was grieved to see the sea gull squished by the side of the road.

An analogy came to mind. Over the years I've met hundreds of Christians like the finches. Life is easy, God continually blesses them and finances aren't a problem. They have plenty of seed or other sources that feed them.

On the other hand there are many faithful servants of the Lord who, like the sea gull, are now squished on the side of the road. They may go to church, they may still sing the songs, but their heart is broken and they feel far from God. Where was He when they were squished? They believed for a child's healing, yet the child died. They waited for God to save their marriage, but they were divorced instead. They went into business, but their partner swindled them. If you hear enough stories and see enough pain, you may find yourself wondering, If God let that happen to Pastor Smith, when will my tragedy come? When will I be squished by the wayside?

Gen. 8:1 tells us that after the waters flooded the earth for a hundred and fifty days, *"God remembered Noah*

... and the waters receded. " Notice that the water wasn't completely gone, Noah was still stuck in the ark, but God had moved on his behalf. Noah just didn't know it.

Noah continued to send out a dove even though it kept returning because there was no dry area where it could land. God was quiet, so Noah waited. One day, the dove didn't come back. Did Noah leave the ark? No, he waited for a word. He removed the cover and saw the ground was dry, but he waited. How many of us would have moaned and groaned and complained to God about what He was doing? Noah waited nearly two more months before God told him to go out.

If Noah had complained during that time of waiting, the joy of receiving God's word, directive and spoken promise would have been tarnished. When the ark door swung open for the last time, Noah's heart was found full of faith. He had not lost heart. Instead, Noah had an unblemished altar and an unsullied word from God, one that he would never forget.

Eleven

The Spoken Word of God

*"Remember your word to your servant,
for you have given me hope."*
—Ps. 119:49

In Gen. 12:1, God gives a word to Abraham: *"The LORD had said to Abraham, 'Leave your country, your people and your father's household and go to the land I will show you.'"* First he is told what to do, and then he is given a promise of what Jehovah will do. With God's word tucked nicely in his belt, Abraham builds altars along the way. He is full of hope as he heads towards the promised land, wherever that may be. But then Gen. 12:10 records an obstacle: *"Now there was a famine in the land, and . . . the famine was severe."* Without receiving a word from God, Abraham heads toward Egypt, that is what seemed best to him.

Maybe Abraham made a beeline to the only place where food was available because his relatives pressured him to do so. All we know is that he simply *"arose and departed"*—without confirmation from God, without a clear word about what he was to do under the circumstances.

Abraham feared that the Egyptian king would kill him for his wife, Sarah. They tell the king that she is just his sister. He gets caught in the lie, is kicked out of the country and returns to Bethel with his tail between his legs. Now he is back where he started from. God is good at taking us back to where we veered off.

There, Abraham calls on the name of the Lord, Gen. 12:8. Several times God comes to speak to him. The Bible says *"the word of the Lord came."* Meanwhile, Abraham calls on the name of the Lord for the next three chapters. All of a sudden, in Gen. 15:6, *"Abraham believed the Lord."* There is a big difference between calling on the name of the Lord in hope, and believing He will do something because He told you He would. God came to Abraham again and told him that his children would outnumber the stars in the sky, even though he and Sarah were childless.

Romans 4 tells us that long before the promise was fulfilled, Abraham was fully assured God was able to do what He had promised: *"Yet he did not waver through unbelief regarding the promise of God, but was strengthened in his faith and gave glory to God, being fully persuaded that God had power to do what he had promised" (verses 20-21).* That made all the difference. God gave him a promise, a spoken word to hold onto. He gave him a vision and a memory-maker. For years, Abraham would sit under the stars contemplating God's promise that his descendants would be as numerous as all the glittering lights about him.

Not too long ago I heard a TV commercial for a car manufacturer. "We are building customer loyalty,"

the ad claimed. How do they figure on doing that? This particular manufacturer has a pretty spotty track record with consumers. When I head out to buy a car, I do so with that knowledge in mind. I'm also armed with a certain set of assumptions: I know I stand a better chance with a new car than with a used one, and I also know from past experiences—either my own or my friends'—which dealers to avoid.

Our loyalty to God should be based not only on the fact that He requires it of us but also on our personal knowledge that we're able to trust Him. To acquire this personal knowledge, we have to make our own memories with God. We need a personal history with the Lord, one we can look back on and reflect upon at times when we most need to be reminded of His faithfulness. In those times in our shared history when God has revealed Himself to me, He has been building customer loyalty. I know, based on the countless times He proved that He will never leave me nor forsake me, that I can have 100 percent faith in Him when the next crisis hits. He won't leave me in the lurch.

same with me

Throughout history, many people have tested God just to prove that He wasn't going to leave them in the lurch either. God's word to them was vital. His promise or direction is what gave them hope.

Gideon was one of those people. One day as Gideon was hiding from the Midianites at the wine-press, the Angel of the Lord appeared to him and said, *"The LORD is with you, mighty warrior."* *"But sir,"* Gideon replied in the next verse, *"if the LORD is with us, why has all this happened to us? Where are all his wonders that our fathers told us about?" (Judg. 6:12).* Not only does Gideon's remark show that he doesn't have much hope, it also reveals two things about him:

One, he's got his own rejection tape playing in his head, and two, he has no personal history with God. How can you have hope, trust or faith in God if you haven't seen Him do anything in your own life? You can't. Your faith is strengthened through God's track record with you, not just through stories told by others. Those stories may help, but they'll never take the place of our own memories with God.

I have seen him work in mine

Then God commanded Gideon to go save Israel. Gideon's first reaction was to look at the circumstances. How could God possibly use him, a nobody from a family of poor nobodies? The Lord promises to be with him. Gideon, unable to believe the Lord would really use him, wanted proof that it was really God who was talking to him. In essence, he says, Prove it. Do some miracle to show You are really Jehovah. If I have found favor with You, then when I return with an offering You will still be here. So off Gideon goes and spends some time preparing a kid and an assortment of other groceries—all the time probably wondering if he had dreamed all this. But upon his return the Angel of the Lord touched the meat with his staff, and a fire consumed it. In the echoes of the wind, Gideon heard the words, *"Peace! Do not be afraid . . . " (Judg. 6:23).*

Not only did the miraculous appearance of fire spark a deep reverence of the Lord within Gideon, but it also signified that God had accepted him. That acceptance was vital if Gideon was to walk in the way God had placed before him. Immediately, Gideon built an altar and called it *The Lord is Peace.* The memory of this experience was instilled in him along with a peace that God would be with him. He believed.

What thoughts must have gone through Gideon's mind as he killed the young kid and prepared the meal?

Will He really be there when I get back? Is God really giving me something of significance to do for Him? God expects us to spend time in preparation for the agenda He has for us. And that preparation time is never irrelevant.

So Gideon, this little nobody, now has a vivid memory that God wants to use him. For Gideon, for any of us, this is one of the most joyful moments in the Christian life, the moment of recruitment into God's army by the commander Himself. Nothing will ever be so thrilling.

But before Gideon has a chance to get too cocky and presumptuous, God gives him a preliminary task before the main event; he was to go into the town and pull down all the idols with his father's wagon. Granted, everybody was perturbed at him, but the mission was successful. Gideon should have been ready for God's call. But he wasn't. He reminds God of His promise, but then doubt surfaces. He has already forgotten the events of the previous few days. Sound familiar?

Once again he wants the Lord to prove He is who He says He is and He'll do what He says He's going to do. Gideon then sets in motion a process of testing God that is now known throughout Christendom as setting out a fleece (Judg. 6:36).

Gideon places a fleece of wool outside and asks God to let dew fall only on his fleece. If the ground is dry, and Gideon will believe Him. God does it, but still Gideon isn't satisfied. After all, going to battle to save all Israel is a pretty scary task if God isn't in it. He demands that God do it again, but this time he wants the dew on the ground and not on the fleece. Once again, God comes through. *always*

71

Is Gideon ready for the challenge? No, not quite. He's had his directive, had his word, had his proof, but God lays a baffling scenario on him. God tells him his army is too big and shows him how to eliminate the deadbeats. He reduces his army from 2,200 to 300. With these odd events fresh on his mind, Gideon goes to the future battle site and spies out the land.

Amazingly, he overhears a man describing a dream he had as another man interprets it; their conversation confirms what God had been telling Gideon all week— that Gideon would defeat the Midianites. Scripture says that when Gideon heard the interpretation, he bowed in worship.

I cried as I read this. It reminded me of all the times God had beautifully reassured me of what He was doing in my life. When the road seems blurry or scary, God can bring Gideon to a place where he can eavesdrop on a life-changing conversation—or He can guide Pat Robertson to sit down next to me at just the right time. Situations like that should make us all bow down in worship.

This shows the importance of having memories with God, either altars or spoken words. They give us hope. Gideon now had complete confidence that God was able to do what He had promised. He realized that God had ordained him to be there at that specific moment so that he would hear that conversation. He could hold onto that truth and that memory even in the midst of battle.

What is God guiding you to do? God has a plan for your life. What instructions has He given you to that path? Are you on it yet? Or were you on it but got off? Has Satan dangled a carrot—some big dream—in front of you that you'll never attain? Maybe he's used some well-meaning Christian to speak a "word" to you claiming that God will do a certain thing in your life, and yet after years of waiting, it hasn't come to pass.

I believe in the gift of prophecy. I've seen it at work too many times to deny its validity. But too often "words" from God were actually the heartfelt, sincere intentions of brethren who wanted to be an encouragement. The problem is that they tacked a *"thus says the Lord"* onto their own wishful thinking. This is why God wants us to get our own words straight from Him.

Moses told the Israelites that they could hear from God but they wanted him to do the seeking and receiving. People continue this practice today, as they wait for their pastor to get a word for them or they run from one conference to another hoping an evangelist has a word for them. I've met countless "squished" Christians who have become disappointed with God because a prophet spoke a word that hasn't come to pass. Many of those prophets actually have a ministry of helps, and their compassionate heart prompts them to give words that extinguish hope instead of building faith.

Once during an altar call I met a woman who was very bitter at God. When I asked her why, she told me that God had told her she would write a book, so she quit her job. Eventually, her husband left her and she still hadn't been able to put a book together. "How did God tell you?" I asked. Looking somewhat confused, she answered that she had attended a conference where a prophet told her she would write a book. I prayed for her and suggested she get her own words from that point on.

In 1 Kings 13:18, God instructs a man of God to return home without stopping to eat or drink. An old prophet approaches him and says, *"I too am a prophet, as you are. And an angel said to me by the word of the LORD: 'Bring him back with you to your house so that he may eat bread and drink water.'* " So trusting the older, wiser prophet—who in fact was lying to him—the man of God disobeys his word and goes off for lunch. On his way home from there, thinking about his full stomach, a lion comes out of nowhere and kills him. He was at the wrong place at the wrong time and would have been spared had he acted on his own guidance and not a "word" from someone else.

Eccles. 3:15 reads: *"Whatever is has already been, and what will be has been before; and God will call the past to account."* Can we do good deeds that don't count? Yes, in fact I'll probably be greatly surprised at some of the wood, hay and stubble I produced because I did what seemed good instead of what was in accordance with God's will.

John 5:29 says that *". . . those who have done good will rise to live . . . "* How do you know if your deeds are good? John 3:21 gives the answer: *"But whoever lives by the truth comes into the light, so that it may be seen plainly that what he has done has been done through God."* So my good deeds have to be done through God. That is why it is imperative to hear a "word."

A promise, or word from God fulfilled, builds customer loyalty. Every time God says He is going to do something and does it, the memory of that occasion helps us to hope, to trust and to be expectant the next time. Before you can have hope or genuine trust that God is going to do something, you have to make sure He promised it to you in the first place. God certainly can send people to us with a word, but more often than not what they should bring is a word that confirms what God has already told you.

In Isa. 42:9, God says, *"New things I declare; before they spring into being I announce them to you."* Many biblical examples support this. At the same time, it is true that God often does things without revealing them first.

I remember a time when God indicated that a change was coming in my life but didn't tell me what. I was getting restless on my mission post and simply wanted a break from the routine. As I read my devotional one morning, I sensed something was about to happen.

The editor's note at the bottom of the page stated, "God is full of surprises." Gently into my spirit came the words, "I have a surprise for you."

Within minutes a YWAM leader knocked on the door and asked me if I would like to accompany a group to Los Angeles for the Olympics outreach. I had to giggle as I answered with a resounding yes!

Twelve

Looking at the Enemy

*"The enemy pursues me, he crushes me to the
ground. So my spirit grows faint within me.
I remember the days of long ago;
I meditate on all your works.
Let the morning bring me word of your unfailing
love. Show me the way I should go."*
—Psalm 143:3-5,8

When God's timing had come for me to go to
Australia in 1989, He had gone before me. My
autobiography had become the top-selling Christian
book, which opened doors for me to preach in hundreds
of churches over the next two years. The whole time I
was there, I couldn't shake the feeling that I would end
up in Minneapolis eventually.

Now that I was there, it was back to the conch
shell. I wasn't prepared for what became a continual
drain on my hope and sense of purpose. I had no idea
of the amount of competition for pulpits. Also, being

fairly new to the ministry of an itinerant evangelist, I was unprepared for the dark cloud that surrounds us as being "God-sent" to the church.

Many a pastor has been burned, and like our Dalmatian, they question an evangelist's motives. It's as if they look for something to be wrong. What kind of car does she drive? Will she wear expensive jewelry? How come she's single? What's the matter with her? Is she really coming to give—or to take?

Soon after renting my apartment, I felt that no pastor in the area wanted to know me. I started to wonder: Can other people block the plans and blessings that God has for you? Can they deter you from a destiny?

The Living Bible translates 1 Sam. 10:26-27 in part like this: *"A band of men whose hearts the Lord had touched . . ."* became [Saul's] constant companions . . . There were, however, some bums and loafers who exclaimed, *'How can this man save us?'* "

Bums and loafers can systematically drain us until we feel like giving up. Trying to bounce back gets harder and harder as we lose our vision and expectancy in pursuit of the desires of our heart.

When God gives a directive, we step out ready to see things fall into place, and before long we can feel no one but us acknowledges His direction.

Scripture confirms that one of the biggest problems people had with Jesus and the disciples was questioning their authority. Who said you can do this? What makes you think God told you? He didn't tell me! (see Matt. 21:23).

Even without the help of demons, people will try to pull you down as a way of elevating themselves. If

↳truth

they aren't seeing God do things, why should you? In Australia they call this the "poppy syndrome." It conveys the same behavior that you find when you place crabs in a bucket without a lid. As one crab tries to climb out, another will pull it back down. The "poppy syndrome" describes the way a person on the brink of success gets bushwhacked (judging and gossip are the primary tools); that way, no one becomes more successful than another.

That's why James warns us about *"jealousy and selfish ambition"* and Paul in Philippians exhorts us to *"regard one another as more important than himself."* Now there's a twist!

As God's mercies are new every morning so was my hope in Him. I knew I had my word about preaching in Minnesota even if no one else appreciated it. God in His faithfulness did provide bookings in small country churches, but with those came small offerings. I was grateful for the job with Jim.

As time went on, I began to feel the rejection of churches in my own city. My pastor, who was from Australia himself, wouldn't even let me preach. He recognized the names of some of the pastors who had written reference letters full of glowing comments about my ministry, but still he wouldn't budge. He said it was a board decision.

One Sunday morning my pastor preached about pressing through with what God has told you to do. I responded to the altar call; the associate pastor's face was etched with suspicion as he approached me. I shared how God had brought me there but that I was struggling in seeing the vision fulfilled. "If you're supposed to preach, then how come you're having such a hard time getting booked?" he asked. To add to the insult, his wife said, "Who said you have a ministry? Get a full-time job like me. That's my ministry."

I felt my body flush with a combination of rejection and righteous indignation. Calmly, I answered, "I can understand why you would say that. There are many women and men trying to push their way into a pulpit for their own agenda. But you don't know me nor my experiences overseas. I am not demanding my right to preach. I am holding onto the word and the confirmations that have brought me here."

With an arrogant look he quoted Prov. 18:16: *"A gift opens the way for the giver and ushers him into the presence of the great."* It would have seemed logical if it hadn't been so pathetic. That verse from Proverbs has nothing to do with spiritual gifts, and yet it is thrown in the face of many a struggling worker for the Lord. The Hebrew word for "gift" in that verse is shachad, and it connotes donation or a bribe, something you give to appease a person or to manipulate them to give you what you want. It's no different from what I did by offering a plane ticket to my leader to get a bunk bed. For other biblical examples of the use of shachad, see Gen. 32:20 and 1 Sam. 25:27.

As time went on, my tail began to lose some of its wag. I was amazed at how many people I met in the church—including returning missionaries—who followed a similar pattern. Their joy and desire to do anything for God had been replaced by a critical cynicism with the local church.

How many missionaries came home and slid right back into the world? How many ended up complacent and pessimistic? What happened? I'm not like them, I thought. I've seen God do too much. I underestimated the very powers I had fought overseas. Little by little they were wearing me down, too.

One day I got a call to come to the pastor's office. When I arrived, the pastor motioned for me to sit down. I didn't know what to think as I watched this distinguished gray-haired man shuffle through what appeared to be my references for speaking engagements.

"I realize you have preached in some of the bigger churches in Australia and have been received by some of my former associates." He looked over his bifocals and grinned. "It just so happens my guest speaker has canceled for this Sunday night. Would you like the service?" I grinned back. God was at work.

Then he opened his Bible and read from Ps. 105:19: *"The word of the Lord tested him."* I immediately got the point. Throughout all my Christian walk, I had been fearless in pursuing what I knew God was guiding me to do, no matter what obstacles stood in the way. I was grateful for my pastor's reminder. I stowed this verse away as a special warning from God, and I was glad I did. Countless times over the next year I had to rely on that verse for the same reason. I had my "word," but a test came with it. Would I give up?

Many of the churches that scheduled me were in rural areas, even a hint of snow resulted in canceled services. By my second Christmas there, I was ready to run. God had gotten smaller, and they had become the giants preventing me from a smooth-sailing ministry. I kept having to prove myself. Why couldn't things be like they were in Australia, where churches actually sought me out? In Minneapolis it was like pulling teeth. Why was doing God's will so hard?

One morning during my devotional time, I began to cry out to God.

In desperation I told God I was going to open the Bible and that I wanted to see a verse that would release me from that city. I opened to chapter 7 of Ecclesiastes. My eyes were drawn like a magnet to verse 10: *"Do not say, 'Why were the old days better than these?'"* I froze. Immediately my eyes fastened on verse 14: *"When times are good, be happy; but when times are bad, consider: God has made the one as well as the other."* God makes bad times? I glanced at verse 8: *"The end of a matter is better than its beginning, and patience is better than pride."* In a matter of seconds, the Word of God had pierced my heart.

Every part of my being knew what God was saying to me. I could almost hear Him asking me, What makes you think you can go anywhere or do anything if I haven't decreed it? I felt ashamed. Little did I know that God really did have a reason for me to be in Minneapolis. Eventually I would see that reason, but while I waited, I changed, part of me slipped away.

God's plans aren't like ours. What seems to be a failure can turn out to have great purpose. God was not only setting my ministry in order, He was also setting my character in order. I remember a spiritual leader saying to me, "Sometimes God takes you from Point A to B to get you to C." What God does through a person's ministry is not the same as what He is doing inside that person's heart. Sometimes one's ministry grows more quickly than one's character, which is what happened to me because of the popularity of my book overseas. Then, when God puts on the brakes to play catch-up, it hurts. If we aren't paying attention, we can become confused and react the wrong way to what He is doing.

You probably know the story of the ten spies who were sent into Jordan to check it out. Eight of the spies came back with reports that the situation was hopeless; there were giants in the land. I was guilty of the same thing in Minneapolis. In my mind, God and His power to work things out for me had begun to diminish, and the people who made the decisions had become the Goliaths. My beef was this: How can you do what God has told you to do when the people you are supposed to do it for won't even ask Him for confirmation? Every place you turn, there is a wall.

During my devotional time one morning I found a verse that particularly touched my heart. 1 Cor. 2:5 reads: *"So that your faith might not rest on men's wisdom, but on God's power."* The wisdom that had been used against me by the leaders was their own. For a time, God had become smaller, and they were controlling my future. Now this loving word encouraged me for quite some time and helped me to turn my eyes back to God, to His power. It helped me to remember my past track record with the Lord and all I had witnessed God do, even defying government rules overseas to make sure that I lived where He wanted me. I knew that God was doing something in Minneapolis. After much heartache and more than a few little foxes of sin running loose in my mind, I realized that what seemed to me to be a roadblock was only a delay that God had manufactured for His good pleasure and His will.

There's a Chinese legend that fits here perfectly. A long way off, in a remote village of a distant land, there once was a farmer who had one horse and one son. The horse ran away and all the people in the village gathered and said, "Sir, what bad luck you have." The wise farmer asked, "How do you know it is bad luck?" After a few days the horse returned with several mares following it. The neighbors came and cheerfully shouted, "Oh sir, what good luck you are having!" The farmer, looking perplexed, shrugged his shoulders and asked, "How do you know it's good luck?" The next day the son was riding one of the new mares and was thrown off, breaking his leg. The townspeople came the farmer and mocked, "Sir, you have very bad luck." The farmer thought for a second and with a shine in his eyes smiled, "How do you know it's bad luck?" A few days later the warlord came to town and forced all the able-bodied men to go to war with him, but he left behind the son with the broken leg.

The lesson we need to learn from this is that we do not always know at the time whether something is good or bad. We must trust and have hope that whatever happens to us hasn't just come out of the blue. God let it happen, and what seems bad could be good: *"As you do not know the path of the wind, or how the body is formed in a mother's womb, so you cannot understand the work of God, the Maker of all things"* (Ecc. 11:5).

We don't know what God is doing. Overseas, my trials in one country prepared me for experiences I would have in another country. My trials in Minneapolis prepared me for situations I would face in the other states where God would lead me.

God had a complete surprise waiting for me within days after I had sought my release from Minneapolis. The Assemblies of God had unanimously determined that I had a proven ministry and therefore qualified for licensing credentials.

All those little country churches had added up. Around the same time I was interviewed on a Christian radio station and was later offered the opportunity to host the show. I had a wonderful time interviewing and gaining insight from some of the top Christian authors and leaders in the country. Now that everything had seemed to click, God released me to leave Minneapolis. Was I ready to start over? Thanks to my encounter with Pat Robertson, I was.

Thirteen

The God of the Bad Times

*" 'Though the mountains be shaken and the hills be
removed, yet my unfailing love for you
will not be shaken nor my covenant of peace be
removed,' says the LORD, who has
compassion on you."*
—Isa. 54:10

During my short time at the cottage in Maryland,
churches opened up in Virginia Beach, which were hours
away by car. I made the drive several times during my
first months in Maryland. The bustle of freeways always
made me glad to be heading home. I was happy where
I was, in a small, quaint town where I saw the same
people each day. It was great after Minneapolis and the
big cities of Australia and New Zealand.

But as I sensed God directing me to move to
Virginia, I remember driving over the long Bay Bridge,
which joins Maryland to Virginia, and enjoying the view.

I pointed off to the left to what seemed to be a non-tourist area by the water. "Can I live over there?" I asked God.

Would you believe that right there by the bay was a little converted garage with my name on it? Within months I was all settled in. But as wonderful as it was, I had no idea it would ultimately become a prison as the walls closed in on me and the peering eyes of demons planned their attack.

All through history the powers of hell have tried to quench the Spirit. Wherever God was raising up a minister for the kingdom, the enemy was hard at work trying to stop him or her through other people. The enemy's forces crept out from all sorts of rocks.

That's what happened to Jesus when He returned to His hometown. He had to perform miracles to earn their trust, and even then some didn't believe. Most had no faith because they had no track record, no personal memories, but also they knew Him only as Joseph's son, a simple carpenter. They did not see Him as the Son of God. He had to give them proof. They needed their own memories.

But Matt. 13:57 says the people took offense at Him, while the following verse says He did not do many miracles there because of their unbelief. Yet in verse 54 they had witnessed His miraculous power, but their hardness toward Him overrode what they had seen. They were too cynical to believe their own eyes.

They had seen Him in action and should have had faith, but instead they had unbelief because they knew His earthly heritage, not His heavenly one. Jesus Himself said, ". . . *No prophet is accepted in his hometown*" *(Luke 4:24)*. In John 4 when a royal official came to Him about his sick son, Jesus replied in verse 48,

"Unless you people see miraculous signs and wonders, you will never believe." So Jesus healed the son, and His miracles made memories.

In Mark 4:35, Jesus speaks a word, a directive, a promise: *"Let us go over to the other side."* But when a storm arises, the disciples get scared and accuse Jesus of not caring. Our Lord rises to the occasion and rebukes the storm, sending it away.

Many believe that this story shows that no matter what storm comes our way, Jesus will send it packing. But that's not the point at all. The disciples forgot not only all their former deliverances but also the word they had received: *"Let us go over to the other side."* Had Jesus forgotten where they were going? Had He changed his mind? Hardly. That one sentence was as much a "word" for guidance as any of the memory-makers Abraham, Gideon, you or I have had.

When people, circumstances or obvious opposition comes, what will you do? Your dreams and visions seem to be moving further and further away. God doesn't seem to be answering your prayer. If you're a go-getter, you won't sit still. Neither will a person who refuses to be labeled a failure.

That is, unless they have lost hope. The heavens are quiet, so why pray? The "Why bother? I quit! I give up!" tape starts playing to ease the pain. Hope defered makes the heart sick.

Pressure from other people can also be hazardous to your faith, your vision. Doing or not doing something based on the approval of others can interrupt God's plans for you faster than you can say "I wish I hadn't done that." It's amazing how easily we can be swayed unless we have been healed from past hurts. Even Paul asked, *"Who has bewitched you? . . . "* *(Gal. 3:1).*

Let's take a look at Saul's downfall. Here is a man that God allowed to be the Israelites' first king. Having a king wasn't God's highest plan, but the people griped so much that God relented and chose one for them.

God came to him with this honor and changed his heart. He became another man. His purpose in life changed, too. He was now an officer in God's army, a general. He was the first to give orders as God or one of His prophets directed. In 1 Samuel 13 we see King Saul in his first battle. His troops were afraid but were told to wait seven days. Then the prophet would return to make the sacrifice, which would release them to go into war. With the clock ticking away, on the seventh day Saul reacted the way many of us would. He looked at the circumstances, and he responded to the pressure placed on him by his men. They were getting restless, and they just might desert him. Saul was insecure—scripture says he was *". . . small in his own eyes . . . "* *(1 Sam. 15:17)* —so when the men wanted their own way, he gave in to them. As he was preparing the sacrifice, which, by the way, was a "no-no" for him to perform, the prophet returned. His fear of man, his pride and his desire to get things rolling himself cost him his job. He was on his way out.

It's sad and disconcerting when we read about Saul. He had such potential, and yet his end was disastrous. We shouldn't be so quick to judge Saul. In many ways our independent natures and our impatience to bring about God's will is no different from Saul's.

There once was a farmer who was sitting on his front porch watching a bird build a nest in some old shrubbery he had piled on the driveway. He knew that in the near future he was going to burn those bushes.

So he went over and knocked the newly built bird's nest out of the bush. The little bird came back and in astonishment cried, "What a drag! Where did my house go?" The bird was sure he had found a good place to live and so he started to gather more twigs to rebuild. When the nest was finished, the farmer noticed it and knocked it out of the way again.

The bird came back and in disgust chirped, "What a bummer! My house is gone again! I guess I'd better relocate." The bird gathered more twigs and built its nest on the other side of the barn.

A few days later the farmer set the shrubs ablaze. The bird was oblivious to the fact the farmer had actually saved her life. To her it had been an unnecessary nuisance and a diversion from her set goals. We need to realize that God may be working behind the scenes when things go haywire or get delayed over and over. Has He blocked or slowed up the fulfillment of His will for a higher purpose? Remember: " *'For my thoughts are not your thoughts, neither are your ways my ways,' declares the LORD" (Isa. 55:8).*

When I think about the walls, fences and gates that seem to pop up regularly, blocking me from doing what God told me to do, I realize that it hasn't just been the difficulty I had getting pastors on the phone for scheduling. Those of us in Christ look to God to bless whatever we may be doing. It seemed that whenever I was finally scheduled to speak or do an interview for a national radio or TV show, my booking was canceled for one reason or another. One year, after a day and a half at the *Washington for Jesus* event, it was finally my turn to speak. As I took the microphone, it poured rain and everyone scattered! Who was making this so

let go & let God

91

difficult? Of course, I couldn't help but think about what I could have accomplished if I hadn't been swindled out of my inheritance. It's no wonder my hope dwindled the way it did.

You see, what I forgot was my own sermons. I also forgot God's track record. The truth is that I have touched thousands of lives over the years and accomplished much for His kingdom. I've seen Him provide abundantly for my needs and even for some of my wants. What if I had all that money when I moved to Minneapolis? God and I both know that I would have run, especially that first autumn when it snowed thirty inches in one night!

Fourteen

Waiting for the Crown

*"All the days of my struggle I will wait,
until my change comes."*
—*Job 14:14 (NAS)*

Unfortunately for Job, each change brought about another grief. But despite the turmoil he was in, he knew that any foreseeable good in his life would have to come from God. This is what he hoped for. David, on the other hand, had a destiny that had been revealed and confirmed but wasn't forthcoming.

In 1 Sam. 20 we see what happened as David waited for his "word," his destiny, to become a reality. He had already been promised by God and a prophet that he would be king. Saul had been fired. Many years had gone by, and Saul, was still holding on to his authority. Saul was insane with jealousy and was determined to kill his replacement. One day Saul's son, Jonathan, told David to wait in the wilderness while he went home to find out just how determined his father was to keep his throne—and to keep David off of it.

David was to wait three days. If it was safe for David to come home, Jonathan would shoot several arrows a specific distance. If the arrows shot past David's camp, that meant it wasn't safe to come back. While he waited, many thoughts must have crossed David's mind. So far in his life he hadn't done anything to perturb God, so certainly God's "word" to him would come about soon.

David also had firsthand experience with Saul, and because of that he might have presumed that even if God specifically told Saul not to kill him, Saul wouldn't listen anyway. Who would win? Just how powerful was God, anyway? Sounds just like my questions.

Look at Isa. 42:3: *"A bruised reed he will not break, and a smoldering wick he will not snuff out. In faithfulness he will bring forth justice."* God doesn't quench the smallest hope. Several verses later, He says: *"I, the LORD, have called you in righteousness; I will take hold of your hand. I will keep you and will make you to be a covenant for the people."* (Isa. 42:6) God will appoint you as an example of who He is and the promises He has for people. You will be a light to those who are in darkness because they don't know Him.

As you grow stronger and more understanding of God and His trustworthiness, you will be able to help others. If you fall to pieces and let rejection fuel discouragement, then you will hardly be able to help anyone else.

You may feel boxed-in right now. Maybe you have experienced the up-down, up-down, hope-deferred syndrome the way I did. But maybe this story about

David's life will give you a renewed hope that all of the promises of God to you are "yes and amen."

In the waiting period Satan has ample time to whisper: It won't happen. Why bother trusting? Give up. But if you have a word, a real word, then God will certainly bring it to pass. Wait with expectant hope. Don't give up. God is good, and trust is imperative. The enemy is out to deplete your confidence in God.

As I think back on my memory-makers, I look forward to my first conversations with my Lord when I go to be with Him: "Hey, how did You do that? I'll ask. I'll never forget the time You did [such and such], and how did You get Pat Robertson and me together at that precise moment?"

While David waited to see where the arrows would land, he might have been thinking something like this: "Is Saul going to blow my destiny? Am I going to have to go live in caves and be on the run with the dregs of society instead of mingling with the upper class in a palace?"

The ironic thing about this is that as David sat behind a big stone waiting to see if he would have to leave and live someplace else, the stone he sat behind held the secret. The stone's name was Ezel, which in Hebrew means "be gone or depart." Here he is sitting behind a stone that stands for "go=away" hoping he won't have to.

But there was nothing he could do but mark time. He sat behind a stone waiting for his destiny. What good would it have done to gripe, cry or be angry? For that matter, why pray? If God was in control of the promise, certainly the son would return with good news. But that wasn't the case. The son returned and shot the arrows that indicated the worst: Go away.

Here we have hope deferred. As with David, sometimes the Son comes to us indicating a new set of plans—a, "No, not now." How do we respond?

David didn't do too well. I believe that at that point he felt rejected by God, maybe for the first time. He probably felt discredited, shelved, separated from God's favor. In this mood he goes to a place called Nob, where the priests who live there are trying to salvage any touch from God themselves.

The priest wants to know why he is there, especially alone. In his dejected state, he lies and says, "I'm on a special mission."

Yet in his heart he must have been weary and a bit fearful in case for some reason God had retracted His grace, so he asks for a weapon. In the true beauty of God's desire to give each of us encouragement, the priest gives David the sword of the giant Goliath, whom David had killed in his youth. The best memory-maker ever! His greatest victory must have surfaced to his heart like a long-lost friend. God had been there in the past, but where was He now? Why wouldn't God bring about the promise?

For David, God's silence and his feeling of hopelessness send him to the camp of his enemy, the Philistines, the very people he hated. The people cheered him on, reminding him of victories past. Yet David, acting out of fear and not faith, pretends to be insane so the king would leave him alone. He stands in front of the Philistine king, wearing the sword of one of their own and acting crazy. Not a very smart move.

David continues on the lam, going from cave to cave, when a horrible thing happens. David didn't know it, but one of Saul's men saw him with the priests at

Nob and squealed on him. Saul in his fury slaughters the eighty-five priests. David's sinful reaction while waiting for God's timing hurt others—many others.

Fifteen

Relinquishing Our 'Rights'

"Be still before the LORD and wait patiently for him."
—Ps. 37:7

Most of us who have a growing relationship with God and have received a special word will also, like David, wait at stones of destiny hoping for the fulfillment of our word—or at least some indication that God is in control.

When a woman is with child, no matter how uncomfortable the waiting period, she can take some comfort in the fact that the baby will come out some way, some day. Yet waiting for the delivery of a baby and waiting for the birth of a vision can be far different experiences, depending on your track record with God.

As I settled into Virginia Beach in 1994 with my Pat Robertson memory-maker tucked away, I had renewed optimism for the future of my ministry and my hope for finding a mate. At least I knew I was in the right town. Things would certainly fall into place. God was faithful in opening doors, although I spent plenty of time on the phone and experienced a good share of rejection, but I kept at it.

There is a principal theme that runs through the lives of our ancestors in the Bible: It's called death and resurrection, and in between is a period called grace. Obviously, Jesus exemplifies death, resurrection and grace perfectly. We also have access to this grace; 2 Tim. 2:1 tells us to *". . . be strong in the grace that is in Christ Jesus."* Yet it's easy to forget that grace extends beyond salvation; God's grace is also multiplied in His desire to maintain you.

It's during this period of grace that we need to understand the importance of relinquishment, the conscious laying down of our dreams and allowing His will to be done. It's during this time that calling on His grace is vital. But too many people—myself included—resort to old behavior and thinking patterns. Some refer to this as the wilderness, others call it a death to self. During this time, many believers become hardened, complacent or simply numb. Unfortunately, it's at this point that our "friends" love to remind us of one scripture in particular: *". . . I am about to spit you out of my mouth" (Rev. 3:16).* Nothing could be further from the truth.

When it comes to the death of self, I was sure I had passed that test already, and I figured that once you're dead, you're dead. But God, was about to teach me that dying to self and to our visions is part of our walk with Him and that no one gets away with trying to avoid this vital step.

While living in Virginia Beach, I began to focus on the fact that I didn't have a social life. Little whispers relentlessly reminded me of all the years I had sacrificed on the mission field and told me that I was due my just reward now.

When CBN announced that it would be holding a major singles conference, I saw a light at the end of the tunnel. I called and was told that some 1900 people were expected to attend, so I sent in my registration check. The day arrived, and I was there early to check out the guys as they came in. By the time the session started, I realized that the only other people in attendance were about eighty older women and six men, though I wasn't sure what planet the men were from.

The speaker, who had been married for some years, was considered an expert on singleness because he had married late in life. I resented the fact that he was chosen to lead this conference. What could he possibly know about single life in the 1990's, especially for a woman in her forties? His lecture was on appropriate dating behavior. I haven't had a date in fourteen years, I thought. Find me a date, and then I'll pay attention to your teaching.

I didn't return after lunch, I woke up with a cold later that Saturday, and had to preach on Sunday. On Monday I called and asked for something in the way of a refund, explaining that I had been led to expect many more people and that I couldn't afford to pay all that money for a teaching that was irrelevant to my life.

The woman apologized, not because I hadn't had a date in so long but because I had been misinformed on the projected attendance. In lieu of a refund, she offered me a ticket for a Benny Hinn event several months later. I thought to myself; go see Benny Hinn? He's married! I accepted the offer. I still believed in the sovereignty of God.

I was obviously not dying easily during this wilderness time. The weeks dragged on, and something inside rose up screaming for attention. I have rights, too, I complained. I wallowed in self-pity, with the emphasis on the "self."

The loneliness was compounded by a lack of any friends or any close relationships whatsoever, and so I, too, became indifferent and withdrew into my own self-centered world. I spent most of my time in front of the TV or wandering through the mall, resenting the fact that I couldn't afford to buy anything. The truth was that I didn't really need anything, and what clothes I did have I had no place to wear.

I kept trying to find a road, real or imaginary, where there would be no emptiness. I was drawn to Scriptures about loneliness that I could easily identify with, like Ps. 102:6-7: " . . . *I am like a desert owl, like an owl among the ruins. I lie awake; I have become like a bird alone on a roof.*"

God was there in my heart, but He was well-concealed unless I was in the pulpit. After all the years of giving, I, like many, had become bankrupt and had retreated to my own solitary confinement. With the Lord of my heart replaced by self, I let His life die in me instead of reaching out to Him and His grace. I kept trying to find a road to take me up, not down—that meant that I should quit ministry and go make things happen myself—a far cry from relinquishment.

be strong in the Lord

STUDY

Sixteen

Anointed—Again—for Ministry

*"Though he stumble, he will not fall, for the LORD
upholds him with his hand."*
—Psalm 37:24

It was late autumn and there was a chill both in the air and in my heart. Two churches had canceled me on short notice—each one because someone "better" had become available, that meant no income for two weeks.

It was just the straw I needed. Grabbing my Benny Hinn coupon, I left the house to go see him even though my, "Why bother?" tape was playing nonstop. On the drive over to CBN, I told God that I wanted Hinn to pray for me personally. If he didn't, I was quitting the ministry and getting a job at Denny's. I was fed up and too tired to stay focused.

I arrived early and was the first in line. I stood there for two and a half hours with at least some optimism that I would get close enough to Benny for him to see me and maybe even pray for me. When it came time to open the doors, the staff opened the other door first! Hundreds of people filed in before me, and I ended up with a seat far from the platform. But all was not lost; I figured that when Hinn called people forward for prayer, I could run down the aisle. I desperately needed a memory-maker to stay in ministry. I wanted God's stamp of approval.

During worship I left to use the ladies room and returned to find that Hinn had invited the hundreds of people who were standing to sit in the aisles. There was no way I could get to the front now. A handicapped woman was sitting on the floor in front of my chair, her twisted legs sprawled out in front of her. I gave her my seat, walked out the door and headed straight to my car, not once looking behind me. I sat there in the parking lot, freezing for almost twenty minutes, and cried almost to the point of groaning. I was crushed. God had not come through.

Had all my complaining and hardness of heart just cost me my purpose in His kingdom? It was obvious I had been fired. Later, as I crawled into bed, the tears kept coming. How did I fall so far when all I had tried to do was help others? "I give up" was the only phrase I meditated on as I fell asleep.

The next morning, as if in a daze, I found myself driving to CBN again. I pulled into the driveway and went into the meeting, which had already started. A woman I had met in line the day before waved me over. She was off to the side but near the front.

Then Hinn asked if anyone in ministry wanted prayer. I thought for a second: Am I still in ministry, or did I get fired last night? I gravitated to the front with hundreds of others and stood there watching this man who had influenced so many people. Now I wanted his attention.

After pacing back and forth a moment, he came to the edge of the platform and, extending his arm, pointed right at me. I froze as our eyes locked. "Honey, you come up here," he said. I was stunned. Who, me? I thought. You must be kidding. I didn't have time to think past that. Several men started moving people out of the way to make a path for me, and then I was lifted up onto the platform.

My heart was racing. Hinn looked deep into my eyes, as mascara streamed down my cheeks with the flow of tears. "What's the matter, honey?" he calmly asked with his thick accent. I took a breath and moaned, "I'm tired. I've been in ministry for years, and I'm tired." He tenderly took my hand as he announced my problem to the audience. "Don't quit. Let me pray for you," he said.

I fell backwards onto the stage. A moment later I was lifted up and found myself staggering. I couldn't stand up, much less walk. I had to be carried down the stairs and placed on a chair. For about fifteen minutes, I experienced the shaking, the crying, the joy. I left there with a new sense of hope and a determination that had long since vanished. I had a new memory-maker. God was building customer loyalty—mine. Yes, God did want me helping in His house, but the devil wanted me out.

For the next year Satan's fiery darts couldn't touch me. I was impregnable with hope and faith and bookings! Charisma ran a story on me under the headline, "Woman minister faces uphill battle." As a result, invitations to preach came in from all over the U.S. This was great

—pastors actually called me! The title of the article proved to be prophetic, as eventually I was back on the phone trying to get services at local churches.

I was like a Girl Scout off to sell her first case of cookies. Her uniform is all pressed, the badges she's earned are on display; she's got a pile of assorted, flavorful delights and her hope and courage are intact; but, everyone in town is either not at home or already has too many cookies in the jar.

Seventeen

Death of a Vision

"For of this you can be sure: No immoral, impure or greedy person—such a man is an idolater— has any inheritance in the kingdom of Christ and of God."
—Eph. 5:5

In my Bible this Scripture is placed so that if you look just to the left another compatible verse sits like a beacon: *"and do not give the devil a foothold" (Eph. 4:27)*. At this time in my life my Bible reading was so sporadic that God never had the chance to remind me of it. I was obsessed with poor me.

Instead of walking in the Spirit I was now in the flesh, and Satan had his foothold—in the form of a man named Mike, sent to replace Jim. Only this time, I would get the attention and the affection Jim had denied me.

I had joined a gym, and on my first visit as a member my thoughts were entirely on physical fitness. I hadn't even done my makeup or hair. I met Mike on the stairs.

He was Greek Orthodox, very handsome and full of charm. Our relationship started with him showing me the ins and outs of the equipment each day, but later it became the two of us talking about spiritual things over lunch. He even started doing the devotional I gave him.

He had no intention of leaving the Greek Orthodox church, and he didn't understand about being born again, but that was OK—God would get him soon enough. He got Jim, didn't He?

I still preached out of town on weekends, but now I had someone to come home to. He left sweet messages on my voice mail, and I found my thoughts were on him much of the time. For weeks he brought me flowers, and I was impressed with his desire to learn how to hear from God.

I made it very clear from the beginning that there would be no physical contact whatsoever. I had obeyed God's rules for fourteen years, and my walk with the Lord was more important than a romantic relationship. After months had gone by, I noticed that my own walk with Jesus had changed. He wasn't the one I thought about all day; Mike was. I had replaced my king with a man.

Two months into this relationship, Mike turned and kissed me. I felt a flood of emotion, feelings I didn't ever remember feeling before, then the guilt hit, and I began to cry. Mike tried to comfort me and stayed for hours, even though people were waiting for him at his house for dinner. He realized the damage he had done. After he finally left, I was numb. I had no sense of God's presence. I was consumed by thoughts that I was now desecrated, profane, deficient, abased, contaminated. I had kept myself pure for all those years, waiting for God to bring me a husband to kiss on my wedding day.

Now that purity was forever gone. Satan and my own need for romance had tarnished my previously unadulterated relationship with God.

I cried all night and met my pastor in the morning. Pastor Kurt had been very supportive of me since my move there. Often when I had a free Sunday, he would schedule me at his church. I knew he thought highly of me, and now I had to admit that for months I had been unequally yoked. I had to face the consequences.

I agreed with everything my pastor said; I agreed that I must never see Mike again. What did I do? I avoided my pastor. It had been fifteen years since I'd had a boyfriend, and I wasn't ready to give this up. How in heaven's name I justified this tryst I'll never know, but when I would return after days of leading revivals, the first place I went was to Mike's arms. Often I was the one who initiated the kissing, which is all we ever did, but I simply couldn't get enough. All the years of loneliness and isolation melted away when we were close, and in a very unrighteous way, he filled the void left by all those who had drained me at the altar calls.

I found I had a new compassion for the many people who had told me about their wrong relationships —usually singles, widows who had also given up on finding a partner in the church. I understood their misguided actions as they waited for God to answer the longing in their hearts.

One day, Mike came to pick me up and leaned forward to kiss me. As I responded, the sound of a loud crash came from the kitchen. I couldn't imagine what could have happened. As I went around the kitchen divider I saw several of my collector teacups shattered in a pile on the floor. Remorse flooded me when I realized my preaching certificate had caused the damage. Somehow, it had flipped off the wall and onto the display case. As I reached down to retrieve it, I heard a whisper—a well-known verse, spoken to Saul by the prophet Samuel:

"... *The LORD has torn the kingdom out of your hands*" *(1 Sam. 28:17)*.

The anguish I felt was indescribable.

Satan comes to steal, kill and destroy, and he had accomplished much of that over the previous few years. He had stolen my joy by replacing it with guilt, and he had destroyed my piety and potential by injecting me with condemnation. I wasn't sure for a long time who had whispered those words of exile, but because I knew I was guilty and had disappointed God, like Eve, I tried to hide from Him. I had lost the intimacy and therefore the boldness to come before Him. Satan had me just where he wanted me, unsure of God's love. I was ripe to get picked off.

Mike left that day deep in thought about the judgment of God and His requirement of obedience. Although I was determined to begin afresh, there was a indolence in my walk and calling that Satan could now use as ammunition. I felt neither worthy of God's love nor commissioned to do His work. Inside I had died. It was only a matter of time before I was bombarded with thoughts of completing the execution Satan had started. I was about to find out in a personal way why some people —including some of the greatest saints—came to a point where they simply wanted out of this life. Like Elijah in 1 Kings 19:4, I would want to cry out: "... *I have had enough, LORD ... take my life ...* "

Ididin 8/2012 + 3/2013.

Eighteen

He'll Do It Again

"But we are not of those who shrink back and are destroyed, but of those who believe and are saved."
—Heb. 10:39

If it is the kindness of the Lord that leads to repentance, is it possible to miss His loving actions due to our own feelings of unworthiness?

When the Lord first comes to Peter, still called Simon at this point, we find Peter cleaning the nets in which he had caught nothing all night. Jesus asks to use his boat so He can speak to the gathered crowd from offshore. After His sermon, Jesus suggests Peter put his net in again. Peter answers, "Master, we've worked hard all night and haven't caught anything. But because you say so, I will let down the nets" (Luke 5:5). Bingo—huge catch! When Peter sees this, he falls down at the Lord's feet and says, "Go away from me, Lord; I am a sinful man!" (Luke 5:8). Can you relate to the feeling of being separated and treated as unapproachable. Little did I know that even to this day I would be excluded socially because people in the church would think, *Oh, she's too busy. She's too spiritual to go to a movie. She may discern my sins.*

I read recently about a pastor who was feeling down and dejected for some of the same reasons. One day as he walked into a store he picked up a piece of paper from the floor. It read, "No man is fully accepted until he has been fully rejected." If some of your friends have pulled away, take the initiative and try to be reconciled. They may need you now more than ever.

But then, we reject God for the same reasons; our besetting sins cause us to fall away. 1 Tim. 1:19 reads, "Some have rejected [their faith and a good conscience] and so have shipwrecked their faith."

Guilt will cause you to depart.

I have a pastor friend who is one of the most gentle, longsuffering people I've ever met. In his testimony he shares that the first weekend his parents left him alone he had a party. Many of us know what that can mean: This one brings that one, and soon you have a house full of strangers who don't care if they wreck the place. They have no loyalty to you, much less your mother's fine china. So the inevitable happened. The party got out of control, and the next morning this seventeen-year-old boy got a big dose of reality. As he looked around the room and saw spilled drinks, cigarette burns and even wedding pictures destroyed, the guilt was so horrible that he left town. For days after his parents returned, no one knew where he was. Loving his parents and not wanting them to worry about his safety, he came home like a dog with his tail between his legs. The house was fairly well cleaned up, but a lot of the damage was irreparable. With tears in his eyes, his father calmly said, "You really hurt your mother and me." This was the catalyst that prompted the son to get saved. His father's forgiveness showed him the true meaning of being in Christ. That was twenty-four years ago, and he's still in the ministry teaching God's grace and mercy.

If guilt causes us to run and hide, then we are the ones who departed—not God. Prov. 18:1 (NAS) states, "He who separates himself seeks his own desire." If we are supposed to be following Jesus and His way, then if we feel guilty and won't repent, we're not going to be in a hurry to draw close to Him.

Many a saint who has been wounded by another is reluctant to open the Bible, knowing God will lead them to a verse on reconciliation and forgiveness. But once we start avoiding the Bible, more guilt sets in since we know we are also evading words from the Holy Spirit. Guilt causes you to shrink back, which is exactly what the enemy wants. When you have no confidence in your rapport with God, how can you possibly come boldly into His throne room?

Let's say you skipped school one day. As far as you know your parents aren't aware of it but you feel guilty anyway—because you *are* guilty. You're not in a really big rush to interact with your parents; after all, they may ask you what you learned that day.

We do the same thing with God after we come under the conviction of sin. We feel guilty, and we assume He is disappointed and doesn't want to interact with us, so we pull away. Plus, if there is a chance we may do this thing again soon, we don't want His correction to add even more guilt.

We cherish the days we walked uprightly and God seemed so close. But now we've suffered a setback. Guilt has caused us to be ashamed to ask for His favor. Why pray? We've lost authority and confidence.

But back to our school days. Let's say you did something that really irked your parents, so they grounded you. But after your sentence was over, something had changed. You need $100 to buy a uniform so you can join the baseball team, but do you now have the confidence to ask your parents for the money? Probably not. You hold off as long as you can. You might do extra chores or even volunteer to play with your little sibling as a blessing to the parent—all in an attempt to pave the way for the favor you need to ask.

Many people do the same thing with God. We expect God's favor when we behave, but once we've have blown it we're not so sure. We try to do things that will earn His favor—give more money to the church, offer to serve in the nursery, all those things that qualify as works.

Because so many of us grew up trying to earn our parents' approval, those efforts are carried over into our walk with God. Disappointing God over and over again can cause us to assume He eventually will stop answering our requests. We're back to earning God's favor. We wonder: *Can I move the hand of God if I do enough to override my sin?*

Scripture tells us that the Lord is good to those who wait for Him (Lam. 3:25). That's not earning favor; that's waiting with a clear conscience. No matter how guilty you might feel right now, you can have the guilt of your sin removed—not only the actual guilt, the charge brought against you, but also the feelings of guilt and condemnation. "For we do not have a high priest who is unable to sympathize with our weaknesses, but we have one who has been tempted in every way, just as we are— yet was without sin. Let us then approach the throne of grace with confidence, so that we may receive mercy and find grace to help us in our time of need" (Heb. 4:15-16).

My dear friend, you will never know how much mercy and grace God actually does have until you draw near. Don't run and hide—physically or emotionally. Think back to your memory-makers, the times God has blessed you. Rest assured, no matter what condition you're in today, He'll do it again.

Nineteen

Revival of Joy

"Because you are sons, God sent the Spirit of His Son into our hearts, the Spirit who calls out, 'Abba, Father.' So you are no longer a slave, but a son; and since you are a son, God has made you also an heir."
—Gal. 4:6-7

In Gal. 4:9 and 15, Paul writes: "But now that you know God—or rather are known by God—how is it that you are turning back to those weak and miserable principles? Do you wish to be enslaved by them all over again? What has happened to all your joy?"

Today, all around the world, worship services that last for hours are filled with people who are experiencing joy, laughter and a sense of God's blessing. What causes them to make merry in the Father's house, of all places? Have they always had the kind of joy that manifests itself with laughter? Some say this new touch from God has brought them back to their first love and given them a renewed hope and deeper understanding that they are accepted by the Beloved.

But how did they lose their first love in the first place?

In too many other churches around the world, people sit in the sanctuary as if they were anesthetized—some because of too many hurts or too little hope, others numbed by guilt and shame. They're nursing weary hearts and holding onto a form of godliness while denying its power (see 2 Tim. 3:5).

All want the joy of their salvation returned, but they're baffled at how to find it again. The sense of blessing is gone. The reason? They backslid. We backslid. I backslid.

The Hebrew word for backsliding is *meshubah*, which is pronounced meh-shoo-baw. When I use this word to refer to the state of some people in the church, I'm not suggesting that we all ended up in the pig slop the way the prodigal son did. In a way, though, we did something even worse.

We *meshubahed* away from the Father. The very wise and experienced Solomon put it this way in Prov. 14:14: "The backslider in heart will have his fill of his own ways" (NAS). The term *meshubah* is used in the context of backsliding in the book of Jeremiah, where God says: "My people have committed two sins: They have forsaken me, the spring of living water, and have dug their own cisterns, broken cisterns that cannot hold water" (Jer. 2:13). They are accused of playing the harlot and adultery, but this is not a sexual accusation. God goes on to make this charge against Israel: "They say to wood, 'You are my father,' and to stone, 'You gave me birth.' They have turned their backs to me and not their faces; yet when they are in trouble, they say, 'Come and save us!' (verse 27).

"Has a nation ever changed its gods? (Yet they are not gods at all.) But my people have exchanged their glory for worthless idols" (verse 11). The Israelites had turned back to weak and worthless things. In a nutshell, they turned to idols.

[handwritten margin note: Present times too!]

We have done the same. I have done the same. I replaced the Father with me. I supplanted His will with mine. Where once we cried out Abba Father, now what we cry out is an echo of self, self, self. Not *Thy* will, but *mine*.

In the story of the prodigal son in Luke 15, the father had two sons that I'm sure he loved equally. The younger son demanded his share of his father's estate. After the father divided his property between the two sons, the younger one gathered what he had been given and left home. In no time, he had spent it all. Just like Solomon, he denied himself nothing that his eyes desired and refused his heart no pleasure (see Ecc. 2:10).

But then a famine comes, and younger son is in big trouble. The party's over, and he comes to his senses. It dawns on him that even the hired help—no, even the slaves—had it better back at his father's house, so he turns around and goes home. Did he repent or change his attitude about life and the blessing that goes with being in the father's house? Did he repent, or did he just respond to his dilemma? Did he plan to stop all his lusty behavior once he was reinstated at home?

Luke says the son's response was, "Father, I have sinned against heaven and against you" (verse 18). This shows that the son is aware of who has authority over him, so he acknowledges God's sovereignty over his life. The father sees him coming and runs to him. The boy says, "I am no longer worthy to be called your son" (verse 19).

Why did the son want to go? He had all the money he could want. In fact, the father's wealth had been bestowed on him. What went through his mind in the days before he left? And why didn't the other brother go? The older brother was happy. What made the younger one think life was greener some place else, outside his father's house? What happened in his heart to make him *meshubah* from his father?

All of us who are born again "live and move and have our being" in Him, in our Father's house (Acts 17:28). He has given us His living. What is it in our lives that might cause us to gather our things and leave the love and security of our Father's home? Jesus Himself asked His disciples: " 'When I sent you without purse, bag or sandals, did you lack anything?' 'Nothing,' they answered" (Luke 22:35). We lack nothing; the Father has given us everything.

I remember lying on a float in Molokai, Hawaii, in 1983, on my first outreach trying to figure out how God would provide the finances for the next leg of the trip. I didn't have much of a history with God yet, but so far He had provided miraculously several times. Into my spirit came these thundering but somehow gentle words: "Don't tell Me how to bless you." In an hour I had access to two thousand dollars. Over the following years God gave me so much, but then something happened. I grew weary in my Father's house. I began to *meshubah* from Him. The reason? Discontentment. I looked at what I didn't have. Key

§

120

When I first signed up with YWAM, I certainly needed plenty of grace, which God generously gave me considering the lifestyle I had come out of. But I hadn't yet learned to relinquish. Like the prodigal son I had come to my senses and knew full well my life was a nightmare. To leave that life was hardly a relinquishment. Giving up my pets was hard, but I was ready for whatever it took to find the true God. However, some months into my Christian walk it was time for God to teach me how to be content, in an unforgettable way. We all must learn this lesson over and over again; I can assure you that the Father will see to it that we do.

In the summer of 1983, I was headed for the airport to fly to Pago Pago, Samoa, when one of the seasoned saints on the YWAM base offered me this advice: "Chris, when things get really tough, don't pray for patience, pray for grace." I eagerly said "OK!" and off I went.

I had just come from years living with all the comforts my heart could want, but now in Samoa I seemed to be headed back into the Stone Age. I was assigned to a house with fifteen other girls—we were packed in there like sardines, our stuff lined up on the floor to mark off our territories. Mosquitoes and all other kinds of creatures flourished because those "houses" had no walls. The ceiling was too high to hang a protection net, so unless you wanted to sleep completely zipped up in your sleeping bag, your face was vulnerable to whatever might land on it.

Since there were no sanitation trucks to pick up the garbage once a week, the solution was to burn it as it accumulated. So, I, who had been delivered from cigarettes and couldn't stand the smell of smoke, had to inhale the burning fumes that wafted into our house. It hadn't happened so long ago that I wouldn't even go to a concert unless I had a backstage pass and could therefore avoid lines for food and pit stops. Here I was in Samoa, trying to find the outhouse at 2 a.m. and standing in line with eighty other people to get a meal. I couldn't even keep a personal stash of food, since that would attract a host of little six-legged vultures, as I learned with my peanut butter sandwich.

One night was particularly trying. Despite my exhaustion, I was robbed of much-needed sleep by the thunderous snoring of a woman at the other end of the room. I waited a few minutes, tiptoed over all the other bodies and touched her gently. All was quiet—for about thirty seconds. I tried again, though what I really wanted to do was stuff a sock in her mouth.

On my way back to bed, I looked out over the village. How far removed was I from all I had known! Instead of mansions lining the hills of my neighborhood in Hollywood, now there were "houses" with no running water, no beds and no walls.

The snoring started again. Obviously, I couldn't yell at her and my sock strategy was out of the question, so as I lay there seething, wondering where all this murderous rage was coming from. *I'm a Christian now. I can't scream. I can't yell. I can't hit her.* So I grabbed my Bible and asked God to speak to me. I knew that by leaving my quarter-inch foam bed I would probably be up the rest of the night, all the next day and into the following night.

Outreach students weren't allowed to be alone, so I walked hesitantly as I tried to find some light not too far from my housing. Out of the shadows came a figure. It was Bectal, one of the staff. I explained my dilemma; he told me to read Hebrews 12. I couldn't wait to sit down and talk with God. That link of communication is *life,* and somehow I knew God Himself would talk to me. Certain verses popped out at me: "Let us throw off everything that hinders and the sin that so easily entangles, and let us run with perseverance the race marked out for us" (verse 1); "Consider him who endured such opposition from sinful men, so that you will not grow weary and lose heart" (verse 3); "In your struggle against sin, you have not yet resisted to the point of shedding your blood" (verse 4).

In an instant, it was as if God was saying to me, *Hey, how hard has all this really been?* Yes, I thought, it's been a paradigm shift, but I haven't physically suffered —not the way Jesus did when the blood dripped from His body for hours so that I might have access to God. That word was the Father's way of saying, *You've done all right in the Father's house. I've treated you well.*

I decided to give up my right to sleep and my right to a quick meal, and I thanked God that I could afford a flashlight to find the bathroom. Even though it was mildewed, I had a foam mat to sleep on. As I rolled with the punches, bit the bullet and quit complaining I began to see God act on my behalf. Time after time, if I didn't demand my own way, God brought deliverance. When I persevered and didn't fight back, He rescued me from innumerable dilemmas.

Too often when times are tough we assume God is punishing us. If we haven't done anything horrible recently, then He's nailing us for something we did in the past. It's pathetic, isn't it? So many of us have this mental picture of God sitting up in heaven waiting for His chance to show us who's boss. As a result, God lavishes us with His mercy and grace as He tries to get us to undo that demented and unwarranted view we have of Him.

In 1985 I returned to Samoa to start up a drama team, and I was happy that God was going to give me the desire of my heart in such a beautiful place. I was due for a week's vacation and had made arrangements to stay in a small hut on the beach for part of my stay there and simply work on my tan. Lama, a native whom I had met during my first visit to Samoa, lived in the same village and helped me lug my stuff along the beach to the hut. I was in the middle of a major struggle. Here I was, a thirty-two-year-old missionary, with a huge crush on this charming, soft-spoken man. That night I apologized to God for my return to old thinking and went to bed early.

The next day I woke up to a beautiful white beach, aqua water and the worst gray sky I'd seen in awhile. No tan today. In fact, it rained the entire week of my vacation. The rest of my time in Samoa was nothing short of a nightmare. As the weeks went by, everything that could go wrong did. Instead of asking God if all this was a punishment, I simply assumed it was. But really, I'd only *thought* about kissing him.

In fact, God was not punishing me. He was doing something else. (The best way to find out what's going on, by the way, is to ask.) God led me to a portion of scripture that brought forth revelation to me personally: "We are hard pressed on every side, but not crushed; perplexed, but not in despair; persecuted, but not abandoned; struck down, but not destroyed. For we who are alive are always being given over to death for Jesus' sake, so that his life may be revealed in our mortal body...because we know that the one who raised the

Lord Jesus from the dead will also raise us with Jesus and present us with you in his presence. Therefore we do not lose heart" (see 2 Cor. 4).

God was trying to change what I thought was the right way to do things. Everything I had grown up learning in my suburban home was irrelevant in Samoa. It didn't matter what side of the plate the forks were placed on, because the islanders don't even use them. All the things that rubbed me the wrong way were a natural part of their lives. I had no right to demand my way in things. I needed to constantly be delivered over to death. Why? Because in order for the Holy Spirit to touch others through me, Chris [Kim] had to be out of the way. If I saw a beggar on the street I, as Chris, could help him. But I can't bring life to him. Only Jesus can do that, as He manifests Himself through me. Good works are good only when Jesus does them through us.

Not long after that, God replaced my trials in Samoa with a wonderful year of ministry in New Zealand. As I left Samoa, I had embraced a new understanding of submission.

The need for relinquishment will surface many times during our walk with God. We'll need to give up things, people, attitudes — in short, what we think are our rights. When we face the requirement of giving something up in order to do the Father's will, we have a choice. We can scream, *What about my rights?* or we can call upon the grace, power and love of the Father and be strengthened. We can embrace His grace in our dilemmas and hard times with trust and faith because self is out of the way.

God's word to me rang true: "The LORD [did these things] to humble you and to test you in order to know what was in your heart, whether or not you would keep his commands" (Deut. 8:2). I saw what was really in my heart, and it wasn't a pretty picture.

Like the prodigal son, I had to come to my senses. I had to get up again after falling. I had to come to the place where I would relinquish my rights and understand that I may never have the things I wanted. I may never have many friends, because mine is an itinerant ministry. I may not have much extra money, because I speak primarily in small churches. I may never have a man to love or a baby with my eyes who will someday call me Mama. It seems the very things I craved from life, those things that I assumed were within my rights to have, may not necessarily be God's will. Can I fight Him? Yes, but not for long.

Strength comes from relinquishment, resting in the Father's house when He tells us to be content, to be grateful and to trust. And like the prodigal son, we will be restored.

Luke 15 shows us that when the son came running home, his father immediately placed a robe, a ring and sandals on the child who tried to leave him. The robe symbolizes our Father's provision. No matter what has happened in your life, you've probably got clothes to wear. But the robe also symbolizes the robe of righteousness, which Jesus Himself provided at our Father's request. We know that Jesus loves us so much that He died for us. But consider this: The Father loved us so much and Jesus died out of His love for the Father, proving His love through His obedience to the Father's plan for Him. Jesus relinquished His rights.

Notice the sandals the father put on his son. Only slaves went barefoot. The son thought his position at his father's house would be diminished because of his rebellion, but by placing sandals on his feet his father was in effect saying, *You are still my heir.* The father underscores the truth that a son is always a son. You will always be God's child unless you choose not to be.

The ring signifies authority. Those who wore a signet ring were people of authority. The signet ring left an imprint that assured the person receiving a document that it was valid; it was as if the sender were there in person to deliver it. Hag. 2:23 shows the importance of the signet ring to the believer: "I will make you like my signet ring, for I have chosen you." Everything God does in our lives is intended to make us like Him. We are like His signet ring; we are His validation. By placing the ring on his wayward son's finger, the father reestablished the child's authority and identity. No wonder his older brother was jealous.

We are ambassadors for the Father as if He Himself were here. We are to reconcile others to Him, but some of us need to be reconciled ourselves—not saved again, but restored in our fellowship. Maybe you've lost your identity, your purpose or your endurance. Maybe you're lost, having strayed away, and you realize life really was better when you were in the Father's will. Do what the son did. When he came to his senses, he admitted his sin and ran home.

This was true repentance. He could have wallowed in his sorrow and simply allowed self-pity and failure to consume his life. Instead, he turned around and went back. Luke 15:24 says, "They began to celebrate." The King James Version translates this celebration as "making merry." I believe this is what prompted the revival of joy and laughter that believers and churches around the world are experiencing. Tears of repentance have been replaced by reconciliation and the joy of knowing that the Father still loves and accepts His wayward children. The wonder of His love etches this truth deep in our spirits: Nothing can separate us from His love.

Thank you Lord for your love!

Twenty

The God of Second Chances

"He carries out his decree against me, and many
such plans he still has in store."
—*Job 23:14*

Part of my frustration on the base in Samoa was caused by the fact that I was convinced these nationals didn't behave much like Christians. One day during a thunderstorm I noticed dozens of frogs jumping all over the yard looking for cover. Some were hopping very quickly, full of determination and with a definite destination in mind. Other frogs jumped sideways, some hardly moved at all and the rest went back to where they had just come from.

The Lord knew I was becoming critical of the islanders, who I thought did things backwards. As I watched the frogs, I sensed God telling me that

Christians were just like those frogs. I took that to mean that believers are all in the same race, but they react to adversity (symbolized by the storm) in different ways. Some Christians know exactly how to respond, others make a side attempt in an effort to cope and still others revert to their old ways. But they're all still in the same battle, looking for shelter from the distresses of life.

Dan. 11:35 states, "Some of the wise will stumble, so that they may be refined, purified and made spotless." Did God make them fall? Of course not, but some of the most humble servants I've met had stumbled severely— and as a result, they could see what was in their heart. This gave God more room to keep purifying them. They see that they haven't arrived.

Even with my complete about-face to the world, what really lurked in my heart surfaced again, and I didn't like it at all. Areas I thought for sure I had put to death reared their ugly heads and took me almost completely by surprise. Because my thoughts and emotions and will were running astray, I succumbed to whatever made me feel better. *happens alot*

Fortunately, God is the God of second chances. Just look at Abraham—when we examine all the situations and tests he went through, we should be greatly encouraged.

Growing up in Ur—which in its day was probably like New York City—Abraham could have had earthly ambitions, given his obvious opportunity for advancement in a thriving city. Despite the fact that he didn't even know that there was one God, much less that he would have a history-changing future with Him, in the midst of the bustle of city life God was preparing him for that day when He would commission him into His service.

It's not clear how or where God first spoke to Abraham, but Gen. 12:1 shows that God gave precise directions: "Leave your country, your people and your father's household and go to the land I will show you." God didn't tell him where he was going. Much of the time we have no idea where we are going. That's why the psychic networks are jammed with calls from insecure people wanting to know the future. God doesn't show any of us the whole picture. The image emerges in stages as we step out and do the last thing God directed. We proceed from glory to glory in physical stages as well as spiritual ones.

A vital lesson in the story of Abraham's journey with God, one that we simply must embrace, is that no matter how far Abraham and his family veered from the path God had set for them, the Lord always drew them back. He did the same for me, and He will do the same for you.

Even though you may not be called to the foreign mission field, you are still called just as Abraham was. He was required to leave home, possessions and relatives, and surrender any thoughts of his status in the world. That's what we now call leaving the world. You are to consider the world and its opportunities as nothing, always pressing on to the higher call of God's plan for your life. And you're to do this even when you don't know where you are going.

Like so many of us, Abraham sets out to do the right thing but somehow, in his zeal to do God's will, little by little his obedience changes to partial obedience and then to compromise. Sound familiar? He was told to leave his father's house, but he brought his father with him. He was told to leave his relatives, but he brought his nephew Lot.

Abraham's first recorded failure was caused by unexpected adversity. Abraham didn't have much of a track record with God at this point, so when the famine came he took matters into his own hands and tripped off down to Egypt, which was not the place God had told him would be "his land."

He didn't trust God to provide for him and his family where they were. His disobedience, however logical, brought with it complications. He was in effect representing the one true God, and yet he brought dishonor to His name when he lied to pharaoh about his relationship to Sarah. Why did he lie? Because he hadn't yet learned to trust God or God's word to him. Out of fear that the Egyptian leader would kill him, Abraham lied and incurred pharaoh's's wrath anyway. He was booted out of Egypt and ended up back in Bethel—the place where earlier he had built an altar. God brought him right back where he started, back to the site from which God hadn't told him to depart in the first place.

Abraham's entourage resumed their travels, and by the time they made it to Hebron his father had decided he didn't want to go any farther. Abraham was stuck there until his father died. It was natural for Abraham to want to bring his father on the journey, but it was also in direct conflict with what God had said. His family did not have the same calling he did, nor did they want to fulfill the mission that this unknown God was laying on them.

Blood may be thicker than water but not when God has given a command. History was held up because Abraham's obedience was incomplete. Presumably, Abraham was doing what was right in his own eyes when he made the decision to bring his father along. But we've already seen that relatives who don't share our vision can end up hindering God's timing whenever our loyalty to them takes precedence over our loyalty to God.

In Genesis 20, once again Abraham lied about his relationship to Sarah. This time God came to the rescue and kept the king from having relations with Sarah. Like us, Abraham experienced repeated failures, repeated falls and, at times, lack of faith. The same is true of his descendants. They were like the frogs; some knew how to hop right into the arms of safety and security, some went sideways or backwards, while others sat still in their numbness.

Just like us, Abraham also had to wait for God's timing. He had been promised a son, but Sarah had not borne him a child. As his natural hope diminished, Abraham gave in to Sarah's insistence that he attempt to fulfill the promise with Hagar, a household servant. Finally a son, Ishmael, was born to Abraham—but not through Sarah.

Abraham had waited almost fifteen years to see his promised son. The problem was that Ishmael was not the son of the promise, and although Abraham's actions were completely outside of God's direct plan, the Lord was merciful to Abraham because He knew his heart. His sins and failures were sporadic and isolated, so God still came and honored Abraham with the promised son, Isaac.

But before Isaac could be given to him. Abraham had a few more tests to pass. One involved his nephew Lot, who probably shouldn't have been with him in the first place. God wants our complete dependence on Him, and Lot wasn't playing by those rules. Their tribes had increased to the point where they each needed some more elbow room, so Abraham and Lot decided to split the land between them. Abraham let Lot choose his valley first. His confidence in God had become so strong that he apparently believed God would overrule Lot's decision.

Once Lot leaves, the channels of communication open up between Abraham and God. That's when Jehovah gives Abraham a bigger vision. The land Abraham got stuck with wasn't half as bountiful as the land Lot chose, but God intended to make up for that. When Abraham graciously allowed Lot to choose first, he passed this test with flying colors.

Abraham had one more test to go through before the promised son would be granted. King Chedorlaomer —who was the Saddam Hussein of his day—sacked the city of Sodom, where Lot lived, and carried off Lot, his family and all his possessions (see Genesis 14). But Abraham, acting on faith, gathered his little army and rescued all his relatives and their belongings.

Chedorlaomer told Abraham he could keep the booty if he would agree to return the people to him. Abraham rejected the opportunity to acquire more wealth and basically told the king to buzz off. "I will accept nothing belonging to you, not even a thread or the thong of a sandal, so that you will never be able to say, 'I made Abraham rich'," he said (Gen. 14:23). In the following chapter, God promises Abraham that his descendants will be like the stars, too numerous too count. That's when Abraham believed.

After all the waiting, all the mistrust and the fear and the outright lies, finally Abraham got the son he had waited for.

But wait—what must he to do about Ishmael, the son he already loves? With a grieving heart—and at

God's command—Abraham sent the boy and his mother away. When Abraham deviated from God's plan, there was strife in his household among Sarah, the servants and the two sons.

Once again, Abraham was required to separate from part of his family. And although Abraham's heart had been torn apart, something inside him still wanted to believe he could trust God completely.

But God wanted to see if He could trust Abraham. Just when it looked as if Abraham was going to have a real family, the family of promise, what did God do? He asked Abraham to sacrifice the one son he had left, Isaac. If he obeyed and killed Isaac, how would he become a mighty nation? God had asked him to kill the most precious thing in his life. With Isaac bound on the altar, God Himself provided a lamb for the sacrifice. What must Abraham have been thinking as he tied the ropes, securing his son for certain death? But Abraham had a track record, a series of memory-makers with God.

As Rom. 4:20-21 tells us, Abraham "did not waver through unbelief regarding the promise of God, but was strengthened in his faith and gave glory to God, being fully persuaded that God had power to do what he had promised." After all, he had the son that had been promised, so the nation must have been next on the agenda.

Once Abraham passed this test, Jehovah broke into the silence and shock of the moment with this affirmation: "Now I know that you fear God, because you have not withheld from me your son, your only son" (Gen. 22:12). And then God repeated His promise to Abraham.

Abraham passed his tests, but his spiritual development and complete hope in the God who keeps

135

His promises was a long time in coming. We're all on a similar journey. No matter what happens, we can be assured that if God is working on us, then He will be at work whether we think we need it or not, and the road will be bumpy for all of us.

Twenty-One

A Weary Heart

*"In him we were also chosen, having been
predestined according to the plan of him who
works out everything in conformity with the purpose
of his will."*
—Eph. 1:11

All that the Father is doing in your life is intended
to bring about your destiny. He opens doors and He
closes doors, always with love and purpose. When we
become discontent in His house, we may easily forget
the love and purpose behind His actions.

Romans and Galatians emphasize that it is the spirit
of bondage that separates us from the spirit of Abba
Father we can't be one with Abba Father if we're in
bondage to our wounds, fears, loneliness, hopelessness,
habitual sins or anger. In order to be one with the Father,
we must allow Him to manifest His attributes, character
and glory in any area of our lives. Otherwise,

the prince of this world will have a foothold in our actions. If Satan can hold us captive to do his will even for a moment, then at that moment we are not one with Father.

Many times I can cry "Abba, Father!" because I have a past track record with God in a similar situation. But in other areas of my life, I allow room for the enemy and in an instant I'm not walking in the right spirit. After too many of those instances, I become unbalanced and before I know it I'm not crying "Abba, Father!" for anything. A wedge has come between the Lord and me, and like the prodigal son I begin to feel unworthy. I not only don't expect God to answer, but I also shrink back and don't even ask. *Same with me*

During my time in Virginia Beach, despite all I was doing for God and His kingdom, I had lost my relationship with Him in the process— mainly due to my complaining and demanding that He answer my prayers. Like Moses, I was about to have a deep desert experience, one that I brought on myself. My insistence on trying to know the future and hurry things along brought me to a point of crisis.

I gave up and figured I'd have to fend for myself. As I sulked and contemplated my lonely future without a bank account, I felt the presence of a spirit that was bent on prompting me to take my life. Day after day this thing hounded me. I would be doing something mindless like trying to decide which soda to buy in the grocery store, and I would feel this oppression affecting my emotions, screaming, *End it!*

How I ever stayed anointed and productive in the pulpit each week is beyond me. My cry to God was to either take me out of ministry or take my life. All my disappointment had turned to anger. How could I continue to trust God? He had not come and vindicated me nor had He kept His promise. Who was I to preach about faith and hope?

Many times as I sat on the platform listening to my introduction all I could think was, *I don't want to do this anymore. Why can't I just sit and have someone minister to me?* I became more and more pessimistic. Deep inside I was annoyed at God because of the inconveniences of ministry. Once the microphone was in my hand, though, I was a different person.

I loved ministry, and I loved seeing people respond to the word of God. It helped to know that all the grief I had gone through was at least helping others. But I had begun to disregard and take lightly the gift and ministry God had given me. It had become a job, and like all the other jobs I'd had, I could certainly quit this one, too. Surely the Lord would understand.

One difficult thing about quitting as an evangelist is that you usually have several months of bookings already set. So when you're in the mood to quit, you still have a long stretch of ministry ahead of you, or if you don't have anything scheduled, after a few months of rest and refreshment, you may decide to start up again but every church's calendar is filled.

My main concern, though, was that if I quit, I didn't know if God would ever give my ministry back to me. I reached the point where I didn't even care about that. In a pool of tears I cried out one night, "I don't even know You anymore".

So I made a mental assessment. I wouldn't book any more meetings until I had my first love back. I wanted God to know that I didn't have to be in the pulpit or the spotlight, even though I knew thousands had benefited from my sermons. What mattered now was being right *with* Him, and that was far more important than doing *for* Him. If the bills didn't get paid, then they didn't get paid. Actually, I was curious to see what God would do and if I would get behind in payments.

After all, I did have a long track record of God's provision but I hadn't been in rebellion, I hadn't *meshubahed* at that time. Would I see Him in a new way? Did He really love me and understand how I felt? Would He come to me?

I had been offered a job at a radio station in Myrtle Beach, South Carolina, but the management at the station kept putting me off. Even though God had told me I would be moving from Virginia Beach to Myrtle Beach, the delays led me to believe I wasn't hearing correctly. It was time to take matters into my own hands.

Several weeks before Christmas of 1996, I went out to find a job. In a way I felt as if a tremendous burden had been lifted, but the word "quitter" never stopped circling my mind. Here I was, at a crucial time in my life, and everything I knew that was of value went sailing out the window.

Instead of watching television preachers, I watched soap operas. Instead of listening to uplifting music, I sang along with the oldies but goodies. The Christian magazines I subscribed to collected dust, and I was afraid to open the Bible for fear of what God would say.

My new job, which took up much of my time for the next couple of months, couldn't pay me in the end. The same thing happened with the next job, and the next. I was so far out of God's will that even my cat knew it would take a miracle for me to get it all sorted out.

In the end, of course, God came through in an incredible way and restored me, just like the prodigal son. But before He did, I had to live out many of the sermons I had written and preached and believed. Had I paid attention to them sooner, I probably wouldn't have ended up with a weary and lost heart. On the other hand, I never would have seen and learned the truth that God is not only the God of second chances but also of abounding mercy.

Twenty-Two

Finding God in Crisis

*"There they were, overwhelmed with dread, where
there was nothing to dread."*
—Psalm 53:5

It's one thing to pray in accordance with God's
will once we have received a word from Him, but what
happens when He is silent? How can we pray in
accordance with His will when He hasn't told us what
His specific will for us is?

The Bible indicates that Jesus did what the Father
told Him. He knew where to go, how long it would
take to get there and why He was going. Or did He? Is
it possible that He didn't know what lay ahead of Him?

One particular incident in Jesus' ministry occurred
after a healing. He admonished the man He had healed
not to tell anyone that He had healed him, but the man
went right out and told everyone, creating such a ruckus

that it restricted Jesus from going to a certain town. Did the blabbermouth prevent those who were destined to be touched by Jesus from receiving whatever He had for them? Did it really matter whether or not Jesus went to that town? Or did He just relax in the knowledge that the Father orders a man's steps (see Ps. 37:23, NAS)? Maybe the disobedient man actually helped direct Jesus to a different place where the Father wanted Him to go. Could Jesus know that healing this man would cement—or alter—His future?

We are a people who want to know our future. *yep* For centuries men have sought ways to know what to do, where to go, whom to trust. Today, we have the people at the other end of the "900" phone numbers to tell us what the future holds, as well as horoscopes available to millions via newspapers, magazines and now the Internet.

Christians are not exempt from this curiosity about the future. We want to hear from God. We expect to get immediate directions and to know the outcome of the dilemma we're in. This is precisely why many people don't seek God when all is right with their world; they don't need to have their future foretold.

When we're in the middle of a crisis, we want to know why. We want to know what we've done to deserve the mess we're in. There are times when we can talk to God until we're blue in the face, and still He is silent. We don't know what we're supposed to be learning through our situation, and we wonder how we can grow and move on.

It's possible, though, that there's a reason for God's silence when we cry out for a word from Him. Instead of seeking Him to find out why we're in a mess, or asking Him to fix the mess we're in, or questioning Him about what He has in store for us before the crisis passes, we need to consider the possibility that God simply wants us to spend more time with Him. He doesn't want us to be in a hurry to leave the King's presence (see Ecc. 8:3).

God uses every crisis for a purpose. But our nature makes us want to know what that purpose is, and we want to know *now*. We pray, *Please, God, tell me what will happen in the future so I'll know if it's worth the pain I'm going through. And tell me soon, because I don't have much time to seek You. Maybe You don't want to tell me, and I can't wait to find out that answer either! I need to know You will fix the problem, so God tell me now what I'm supposed to do.*

We want the most beneficial result in the least amount of time. Unfortunately, too many of us hold on to the memories of times God didn't provide a suitable outcome, when things seemed to have gotten worse. In the silence, we forget the times He did come through. When He's quiet we just go numb and wait till the storm blows over so we can evaluate how God handled the crisis. Do we approve of His actions in the midst of our trauma? Is He as faithful as we once thought He was?

In Ex. 17:1-7 the Israelites have followed God's leading to a place called Rephidim, after going from place to place once they left the wilderness called Sin. They fully expected a land flowing with milk and honey —and water. But, much to their dismay, there was no water at Rephidim. They griped at Moses until He asked God what to do about their dilemma of thirst. God told him that if he would strike a certain rock, water would flow from it. Moses is given both his direction and its outcome. So far so good.

But look at the name Moses gives this location: "And he called the place Massah and Meribah because the Israelites quarreled and because they tested the LORD saying, 'Is the LORD among us or not?'" (verse 7). Instead of patiently trusting and exercising their faith, the Israelites questioned God's provision. There's no water, so, well, let's just blame God.

Psalm 106, beginning with verse 7, describes an earlier dilemma involving these same people. The Jews have pharaoh's army hot on their trail. They accuse Moses, who is God's spokesman, so in effect they are accusing God: *Did you bring us out here to die? Is this the reason for our crisis? We have pharaoh's army behind us and a huge sea in front. Is Jehovah with us or not?*

In Ex. 14:13, Moses told the Israelites, "Do not be afraid. Stand firm and you will see the deliverance the LORD will bring you today. The Egyptians you see today you will never see again." He told them what to do (*don't fear*) and the outcome (*you'll never see them again*). But here they are at Rephidim, between a rock and a hard place, and they seem to have forgotten the lesson of the Red Sea. Not only does God not want His people to gripe, complain and seek Him only when they want answers, but also He wants them to simply learn more of Him, to exercise their faith for no other reason than to know God better. That is the way our faith deepens, by seeing a side of God we haven't known or experienced.

As they stood on the shores of the Red Sea, the Israelites expected the worst. They lacked memory-makers with God. Their still-sore backs reminded them of the whippings they received as slaves. But at Rephidim, they were without excuse.

As we know, "faith is being sure of what we hope for and certain of what we do not see" (Heb. 11:1). But we need to assess why we're birthing new faith: Is it only to solve a problem or to change our circumstance? Or is it simply the way to have God impart more of Himself to us?

I am sure that as the Israelites were passing through the enormous walls of water, the mind games were horrendous. *Did Moses really want us to come through here? Did he mean I wouldn't see those Egyptians again because I'm going to drown any minute? If I can get through here, certainly pharaoh can too.*

The very thing the Israelites were afraid of, the Red Sea, was the very thing that saved them, as God closed the sea on pharaoh's army. They were afraid of what was behind them and afraid of what was ahead, because it was unknown. *we always fear the unknown*

In that crisis, they should have learned more about God. But if they did, they didn't retain the information for very long. God brought them safely to the other side, provided manna for them and fixed a smelly but healthy lake so they could drink from it, all to show He could be trusted. For a while, they sang about how wonderful and faithful God was, but their praise was short-lived. Ps. 106:7 indicates that "they did not remember [the Lord's] many kindnesses."

Lord, help me to remember and to never forget how you saved me!

147

Twenty-Three

Passing through the Deep

"He rebuked the Red Sea, and it dried up; he led them through the depths as through a desert."
—Psalm 106:9

One thing the Israelites did not realize—and this is something we need to understand as we wait on Him—is that God could not tell them the reason behind the Red Sea miracle. He did not part the waters just to show His power or to get more people to trust him. While they were stopped dead in their tracks, God knew they had another wilderness ahead. By taking them through the depths of the Red Sea—what the King James Version calls "the deep"—He was preparing the Israelites for another deep situation.

What if God had told them, or us, *Go through this mess, because I've got a worse one for you later.* Would they embrace the next mess or hightail it out of there the opposite direction?

The next crisis hit them where it really hurt—in their stomachs. To compensate for the lack of food, God provided manna from heaven, which in turn provided excellent nutrition for a population that would otherwise starve. Once again, the Israelites allowed their human nature to take over. At first, they were surprised by and grateful for the manna. But after a while, they wanted something else. They began to lust for the food they left in Egypt, the land of their slavery. Believers today are certainly no different; it's just like us to praise God for a new job and a year later demand deliverance from it.

The Israelites, forgetting His works, did not wait for God's counsel but demanded that God send something new to eat. In this wilderness, they wanted what they thought would be good for them. He granted their request; as a result, a "wasting disease" spread among them (Ps. 106:15).

How many of us waste away in the wilderness when God would rather we get ready for the future by learning more about Him? Our ingratitude and complaining causes bitterness and anger toward the one we think has caused our situation. The Israelites did the same thing; they turned right around and lashed out at both God and Moses (*Hey, Moses, I could do a better job hearing from God than you can!*).

One of my landlords had at one time been a diplomat for the Iranian government. During the hostage crisis in 1980, he was assigned to the Iranian Embassy in Chicago. One night he woke up to find twenty FBI agents and members of the news media surrounding his house. He was told that he was being deported the following day. His seventeen-year-old son was already in custody; the American government had chosen to make an example of him to show the world that the U.S. was taking action against Iran.

His wife, a sweet little woman, was suffering from cancer. The treatments were working, but the pain was unbearable. Mrs. Matin looked at her husband—the way Job's wife probably looked at her own husband—and waited to see what he would do. They had been high school sweethearts and knew each other inside and out. She tried to predict his response: *He won't be able to get us out of this. The man I depend on, the man I trust— what can he possibly do now other than give in and lose his temper?*

The man she thought she knew did something she never counted on. Mr. Matin went to the Old Testament and said, "God, if You're really there I need to hear from You." Understand, these people were diehard Muslims by birth, but Mr. Matin didn't believe in anything at this point in his life. Yet in his crisis he went to what he calls "the Holy Book" and opened to the story of Noah. This verse was what he laid his eyes on: "The Lord said to Noah, 'Go into the boat with all your family,'" promising to save them (TLB). Mr. Matin then did the unthinkable: He went back to bed. His wife, the news media and the FBI couldn't believe it.

Mrs. Matin was nearly in shock. Not only had she seen a different side to a man she thought she knew so well, but also she saw and heard him turn to God and believe the word He gave him. Her respect and love for her husband deepened in a moment; her sense of security changed forever. In her Red Sea experience, Mrs. Matin learned a new lesson about the man she thought she knew better than any other.

As I look back on how God brought me through one deep sea after another, I can recognize His grace and mercy. I saw a new side of Him. I learned of *Him*. I saw the truth of God's love for me. I learned lessons I couldn't have learned any other way.

If the prodigal son hadn't left and come home with his tail between his legs, he wouldn't have known his father's unconditional love. I wouldn't have either. That doesn't mean you should wander off so you can see what it's like to come back, but the many, many people who have lost their first love need to know He forgives. Come back, and you will know more of *Him*. *yes Lord*

Years ago when I was in Fiji, I had planned to spend a few days on one of the sandy white beaches pictured on travel posters. But when the day arrived, a huge storm prevented me from going. I got depressed but decided to try and persuade God to blow the storm away. I opened my Bible and read Phil. 1:12: "What has happened to me has really served to advance the gospel." So I accepted my situation, because my future had been foretold. I knew there was a kingdom purpose in this. What I didn't know was that God was about to take me into the most anointed and powerful two months I ever would have in that country.

That very night I received a phone call from an ambassador's wife. "I had a vision of you, and I need to meet with you tomorrow," she said. Word had gotten around about this "foreigner" who had a deliverance ministry, and my hotel room became a center for ministry day and night. God was teaching me how to cast out demons. I saw the overpowering authority in the name of Jesus as demons came crying out.

Two weeks into this I discovered that a group of about thirty men and women knew that I was coming to the area through a word they had received. They knew even before I got my direction to go; they had been told to "wait for the foreigner." God took me to a place in Him unlike anything I had encountered before—and all because He didn't blow the storm away.

I was only three years old in the Lord, but God was demonstrating the power of the name of Jesus through me. The responsibility was awesome, the thrill incredible. Even when demons challenged me, the fear I felt in the natural couldn't hold a candle to the oneness I experienced with Christ. I was doing the works that Jesus Himself had done. What a privilege!

In Ps. 6:9, David writes: "The LORD has heard my cry for mercy; the LORD accepts my prayer." How did he know? How does anyone know, especially when they don't see an immediate answer? It all goes back to that revelation, that quickened word through which God imparts Himself to you.

In Psalm 6, David cried out to God because of all the enemies he had; he knew God had heard his cry to deliver him. He didn't know how He would do it, but that was OK; God had somehow given him assurance. There's no indication that God spoke to him, so it's likely that he simply received an impartation of God, an impartation of faith. He knew that he knew that God was with him.

In most of David's psalms, he calls for the Lord's strength to help him, but in Ps. 22:19 David says this: "O my Strength." He isn't just asking God to give him strength; he is calling God Strength itself. God *is* his strength; strength is an attribute of God being imparted to David.

Often in Psalms we read of the Lord bringing peace to His people. But in Ps. 109:1 we read, "Hold not Thy peace" (KJV). This reveals an impartation of peace, the very life of God that shows who and what God is. God is peace itself, not an emotion (see Phil. 4:7).

Most of us, at least once in our Christian walk, have asked God to give us His love for someone we can't seem to love, haven't we? We run to and fro at conferences, seeking His power, fire and anointing. So why not ask Him for His peace, His strength, an impartation of Himself?

Galatians exhorts us to live by the Spirit. Is that what the Spirit gives us—or is it the very impartation of the Holy Spirit Himself? When you're hurting you can go to a friend for comfort. Your friend can say things that will help you feel better, maybe even optimistic. But that is not the same as God's life manifesting His spirit to bring forth a part of Him. The way to learn more of Him when facing a crisis is to allow God to impart Himself.

At that moment of impartation, we do not need to know the why, the what or the when. We need to know *Him* and the power of His resurrection.

Twenty-Four

Bless This Mess

"I went in response to a revelation and set before
them the gospel that I preach among the Gentiles."
—Galatians 2:2

Have you ever seen one of those signs that reads
"Bless This Mess"? They're usually found in a junky
room of the house, and the sign expresses the owner's
attempt at seeing the humor in the situation.

But "bless this mess" is also how some of us pray.
There have been times when I would try to tackle a
problem while eating a bowl of corn flakes, thinking
through the possible alternatives to my plight, and then,
when one solution seemed to override the others, I'd
offer my idea to God in a "bless this mess" sort of way.
I assume He will do what I asked since it was the best
idea out of the lot, and because it's an obvious solution.
I also figure it came from Him. I can't wait to see this
mess sorted out quickly, the way I believe He's going
to do it.

yes It's at this point that many of us try to muster up the faith to believe. We name it and claim it. We might even venture to fast for it. It's such a logical solution to the problem that we just keep waiting for God to come through. Then we wait some more, and some more. It never happens. What went wrong?

What went wrong is that the solution wasn't birthed from above. It didn't come as a revelation of the Spirit. It wasn't His will.

The Bible is full of obvious promises from God, including specific ones that He has already fulfilled in our lives such as His promises that He will provide food and shelter, that He'll never leave us, that He gives long life to those who honor their parents. But through the lives of various people in the Bible we can see that often when God shows up to give a word, He has something for the saint to do.

When He told Peter through a vision to go to Cornelius's house in Caesarea, He had a purpose. Did God speak to him to fulfill Peter's own desires, or God's? Did He give him a vision so he would have more faith to claim a better house, a bigger car, an easier life? No. He spoke guidance, direction and purpose.

In Gal. 2:1, we see that after fourteen years God sends Paul to Jerusalem for a purpose. Did Paul want to go? Not necessarily. Would it help him personally with his family life? No indication of that, either. He went because he had received a revelation.

We in the church today need to start focusing our attention on words of revelation that God gives for a purpose. In Gal. 1:15-16, Paul writes, *"But when God, who set me apart from birth and called me by his grace, was pleased to reveal his Son in me so that I might . . ."*

Might what? Go to heaven, get a good job, get rich, always be healthy, get married, have perfect children?

No! God spoke a directive. God wanted to use him for His glory, to preach Jesus among the Gentiles.

I am convinced that much of the church today is at a standstill spiritually because the faith of the brethren has been crippled by unanswered prayers—prayers that never would have been prayed had the believer sought a word from God first. God always has a purpose in giving a word, and He always has a purpose in answering a prayer.

Countless Christians have stopped their efforts at personal evangelism not only because of the fear of rejection, but also because some of their loved ones aren't saved. They erroneously claim Acts 11:14—"You and all your household will be saved"—even though this is a specific prophetic statement about a specific family.

It's certainly true that God does not want anyone to perish, but you need to get your own word for your own family. At one time God gave me a very specific word about what was blocking the salvation of one of my family members. When I prayed in response to that revelation, she led herself to the Lord. I was thousands of miles away and had no personal involvement in her salvation experience.

We also must learn to separate our personal prayers from kingdom prayers. Too many believers aren't praying kingdom prayers because they haven't seen their personal prayers answered. Many God-fearing brethren have simply ceased trying to do anything for God because the few prayers they've been praying, about finances or a loved one's salvation or a personal healing, haven't been answered. Some people have even gone so far as to use Acts 11:14 as justification for their refusal to witness, waiting instead for God to do all the work in saving the household. What if I had done the same? what if I had just sat back and never prayed the word God had given me?

They aren't looking to see what God wants them to do personally for His kingdom. What is the point of words or revelations, after all—so I can prosper? Maybe. Learn more of the Bible? Probably. Grow more in Christ? Obviously! The truth of Matt. 6:33 is still truth for today: "But seek first his kingdom and his righteousness, and all these things will be given to you as well."

If you aren't seeing your personal desires fulfilled, don't stop praying kingdom prayers. Private wants and kingdom wants aren't the same. Praying for others gives you significant input into their lives and into the future of the kingdom.

Think about the stories you've heard missionaries tell. They go on and on about all they see God do. Then you look at your life, and you figure God isn't answering your prayers because you aren't doing anything for Him. Well, in a way, you're right. We have become much too selfish in our prayers, in asking God to bless us rather than asking Him to tell us our gift, our place and our purpose in Him.

We have an interesting example of this in the events of a day in the life of Joshua. One day, one decision, that wasn't birthed from above. The result: significant repercussions.

In Joshua 9, God told Joshua not to make a pact with those who lived in the surrounding areas. But a nearby tribe of Gibbonites decided they wanted to be allied with Joshua. They approached him, pretending they had come from a very far distance by carrying moldy bread and wearing shoes with holes in them. They even implied that they had heard great things about the God of Joshua.

Josh. 9:14 states clearly that Joshua and his men "did not inquire of the Lord." They looked at the circumstances and assumed the Gibbonites were telling the truth. They made a binding covenant with the tribe, and the aftermath was a bit of a bloody mess.

In David's life, we see not only that we can be misled by the counsel of others, but also that something that may appear a glorious thing to do for God isn't always His will.

In 2 Sam. 7:1, David, all settled down in his palace, called on the prophet Nathan and essentially said, *I have a nice house, but God doesn't.* Nathan mistakenly answered, "Whatever you have in mind, go ahead and do it, for the LORD is with you" (verse 3).

But that night God said to Nathan, *Have I ever told anyone in all of Israel I wanted a house? Tell David that the Lord will make a house for you and when you're dead, your descendants will build a house for my name.*

Nathan—sheepishly, I would assume—relayed the message. Then David went before God and said this: "What more can David say to you? For you know your servant, O Sovereign LORD" (verse 20). (Translate that: *Hey God, I meant well. I wanted to do it for You.*)

Yes, God does know the great things we want to do for Him, but sometimes those great things come with our "bless this mess" prayers, as they did in this case. Like many contemporary Christians, David seemed to believe that doing great things for God involves us doing the things and God either blessing them or not blessing them.

David thanked God for the word that had come forth and that in God's goodness He let David know that David's great idea was outside His will. At this point, David claimed the word: "And now, LORD God, keep forever the promise you have made concerning your servant and his house. Do as you promised, so that your name will be great forever" (verses 25-26). This is one of the most intimate conversations recorded between David and God. David acted on this revelation and surrendered completely to the word he had been given.

Now he can pray according to God's will, even if it means his great idea will be passed on to someone else to bring into reality. Someone else besides David will now have the opportunity to bless the Lord. This shows tremendous humility. In the end and with God's blessing, David was permitted to gather the materials for the house, but he never saw it completed. Instead, it was his son who would build it. The irony is that Solomon was David's son with Bathsheba, and we all know he never should have been with her in the first place. Interesting.

One time after a service a couple stood in front of me at the altar, the wife in tears, the husband with a confident expression on his face. This man gloated over the fact that God supposedly had spoken directly to him: "I'm supposed to divorce my wife and marry my old girlfriend so I can bring her to Christ."

"Have you ever read your Bible?" I asked. Spirits can make us think that God is somehow placing His blessing on our lusts. That's why it's imperative that we learn to discern who it is that's giving us spiritual guidance. Hundreds of Christians have told me that God never speaks to them, or that if He does, they don't understand what He's saying. I'm amazed how many people say He hasn't spoken to them in years.

In June of 1984, I diligently sought a word from God about whether I could go to Samoa and serve Him there. Because of previous commitments, I knew September would be the earliest possible launch date. Being the planner I am, I wanted to know where I would be in the fall.

As I sought Him I got no answer. I fasted one day, two days; to me this was a real sacrifice. By the third day, I was starving and told God I needed an answer. I opened my Bible to Ps. 46:10, which reads, "Cease striving." Well, I thought it said "cease starving," so I decided that if He wasn't ready to tell me, I'd might as well wait on a full stomach. Why go through this torture?

I was too young in the Lord to understand that He plans my steps and that fasting is a part of discipleship. I already knew that I would be ministering at the Los Angeles Olympics for two weeks in August. I was excited about that, but still I wanted to know what would happen in September. I had an opportunity to stay in L.A. a little longer after the games were over and jumped at the chance, since I had old friends in the area.

As I prayed, though, I read: "And when they asked him to stay for a longer time, he did not consent" (Acts 18:20, NAS). This was a clear no from God, so I booked my trip for only the two weeks as originally planned.

While I was in L.A., the Stones' manager tracked me down at a church, where I was sleeping on a bathroom floor—a far cry from places where we had rendezvoused before. I wanted to spend time with him, but in obedience to God I returned to Hawaii.

Within two days after I returned, I met a girl who felt she was all right with God. As we spent time together, she realized she had nowhere near the rapport I had with God, and she gave her life to Christ. A local church had planned a massive Bible giveaway but couldn't find anyone to head up the effort. This girl, fresh in her new life, put the whole thing together. At the end of August, she handed me a plane ticket to take me back east, saying God had directed her to give it to me.

That September, I had the most glorious time renewing old relationships and allowing my relatives and old friends to see how much I had changed. Back in June, no matter how much I begged or fasted, God couldn't tell me where I would be in September, because first I had to be obedient in August. It would have been very easy to rationalize staying one more day in L.A., but had I done that I never would have met the girl. She ended up working at CBN and became a real trouper for God. Would she have met the Lord if I hadn't met her? Who knows? But no matter what, the ticket she gave me proved to be a wonderful blessing from God.

When it comes to hearing from God, there are many books on the market to help you learn to discern His voice. But I want to share what I have learned. As I describe the ways God has spoken to me, see how many ways similar He has already spoken to you.

First, if you're not born again, the only thing God will tell you is to repent and believe in Jesus for salvation. Next, understand that if you are saved but feel unworthy, guilty or condemned when you go before Him, those feelings are not from God. true

Ps. 66:18 says, "If I had cherished sin in my heart, the Lord would not have listened." If what you are sensing is the conviction of the Holy Spirit regarding a specific sin in your life, confess the sin, trust that you are forgiven and wait to hear His word to you. Any condemnation you may feel after that is clearly satanic, so use your authority in Christ and tell the demons to shut up. Then trust God to come to you with His guidance and encouragement.Having time alone with God each day is vital. The enemy wants you to stay away, so remember—you can come boldly into His presence. He wants the conversation!

When we're in His presence, it's easy to let our thoughts wander to other things. If thoughts pop into your mind about things you need to do, just write them down quickly and go on with God. Too many people end up skipping any time with Him because they've been told they have to pray in some set order, like *praise Him for fifteen minutes, then He will show up. Pray for the nations, then present your personal request to Him.* Yes, God does inhabit the praises of His people, but you don't need to spend fifteen minutes telling Him how glorious He is in order to come into His presence. When your life is falling apart, do you really have the time to worry about prayers for those in Nigeria? Start out simple, and as time allows you'll find you will want to pray about those other things as well.

Just thank Him for all He did for you the day before, and be sure to write it down. As your heart softens, the praise in your spirit will automatically begin.

Twenty-Five

Hearing from God

*"To one there is given through the Spirit the message
of wisdom, to another the message of knowledge by
means of the same Spirit."*
—*1 Corinthians 12:8*

If each of us is to drink from the same Spirit and if
each of the manifestations of the Spirit is for the
common good, then certainly God will communicate
specific words to His children for specific situations.
So let's look at some of the ways God speaks to us.

Bible Reading

God will speak through our daily reading, which is
why it's important to read daily! Let's say you are
systematically reading the books written by Paul. Next
on your list is Galatians. Heavy on your heart is the fact
that everyone at work has made their quota of sales for
the month—everyone, that is, except you. You feel like

quitting. You're moving into a grumble mode. As you read Galatians 6, you eventually hit verse 9: "Let us not become weary in doing good, for at the proper time we will reap a harvest if we do not give up." The verse leaps off the page and into your heart. In an instant, you sense that God is saying, "Don't quit—you will make a sale soon."

This is a specific word, one that you needed at just the moment. It gives comfort, direction and promise, and some call it a *rhema* word. A rhema word is a portion of Scripture that comes alive for you because the living Holy Spirit is saying it to you. On another day, you might read that same verse and it would simply sound like a good verse to claim on a depressing day.

I like to call this a *revelation word*. The other ways that God can speak to you, whether to provide information, comfort or direction, are also *revelation words*.

God also uses *rhema* words from Scripture as a personal correction for that moment. He did that to me one time in particular, and when I look back on the incident now, I'm ashamed to admit what I did.

For a while, when I would give an offering, I would give cash. I didn't keep a record, because I knew God knew and I didn't really care. I gave spontaneously and generously. But because I paid in cash, the church leaders had no way of knowing that I had given anything. Then one night I found out that the pastor looked over the books to see the amount individuals had given. I had been in that town for several months and had given a fairly substantial amount, but the pastor wouldn't have known it.

So one evening, I purposely got an offering envelope and filled out my name so I could get credit for it. As I was about to put my money in, I saw a twenty-dollar bill already in the envelope. By this time, the usher was long gone, so I just put my money in and added the twenty dollars to my total.

Before I went to bed that night, I opened my Bible to Galatians and picked up where I had left off earlier. As I read Gal. 1:10, that verse spoke to me as it never had before: "Am I now trying to win the approval of men, or of God? Or am I trying to please men? If I were still trying to please men, I would not be a servant of Christ." Now that verse in context has nothing to do with what God busted me for. But when He breathed on it that night, it brought special revelation to me—not to mention embarrassment. Remember, the word of God is alive, and His Spirit is alive in you. The two unite when He gives a word.

Scripture References

Sometimes in answer to the current question of your heart, God will point you to an exact verse. One time when I was under a certain amount of pressure about moving, I knew I needed an answer that day. Clearly, from deep within, I heard 2 Tim. 4:6. At that point I hadn't memorized much Scripture and didn't have a clue what it said. But I turned to it with anticipation and read, "The time has come for my departure." Because I had received a word, I moved with an unexplainable peace and optimism.

Sometimes He'll give an exact reference, while other times He'll simply lead you to a specific book of the Bible. Once, in New Zealand, I was asked to speak at a youth rally led by Billy Graham's son-in-law. I hadn't done much public ministry at this point, and the thought of standing in front of thousands scared me. But what

IMPORTANT

an opportunity to share my testimony! I had to leave the country for three months because of my visa restrictions but upon my return I called to confirm the date and was told the speaker roster was already filled. I was hurt and felt rejected but decided it was worth it to try to get God to change their minds.

Then it occurred to me that I would only be setting myself up for more disappointment if it wasn't God's will for me to speak at the event after all. So I asked God about it and very clearly heard the word Malachi. With the help of the index, I found the book and started reading: "'*I have loved you,*' says the Lord" (Mal. 2:2). Well, that was encouraging but too general. Was I going to speak at the rally or not? That's what I wanted to know. As I read verse 5, though, I was flooded with a rush of anticipation: "*You will see it with your own eyes and say, 'Great is the LORD.'*" I flipped the page and another verse stood out: "*And you will again see the distinction between the righteous and the wicked, between those who serve God and those who do not*" (Mal. 3:18).

It was so powerful. I knew He would do it. Four days later the rally organizers called and asked me to speak.

The people I met that night not only were instrumental in publishing my first book but also in helping me establish a ministry in Australia years later. One man I met that night opened the way for me to preach for the very first time and through that confirmed what God had told me when I was a baby Christian: "Do the work of an evangelist."

The Still, Small Voice

God also can bring to your mind a verse you've read before but never took much notice of. As missionaries, we always had to pray in our airfares in order to participate in outreaches. At one time I had six weeks to come up with a thousand dollars for a trip. Most of the team members had received their money from various sources, but I had no one to turn to. In fact, for years I had no regular support at all. So I asked God when some money would come in for me. What came to me was this: "*And Jesus raised him up on the last day.*" The last day!

That was my word. When the last day came, a businessman came into the office, looked over the list of those with insufficient funds and picked out my name. He paid it all, and to this day I have no idea who he was. I didn't have to worry about the money over that six-week period, because God had given me a word— the last day! God always comes through

God speaks to us through what we call a still, small voice. Nowhere in Scripture have I found an example where God spoke inside someone. There are examples of directions being given by way of dreams and visions, but I don't know of any time when a direction was given that was spoken from the inside. Jesus knew God had heard His prayer before raising Lazarus from the dead, but we don't know what God said to Him or how He said it. Often believers will say "God told me" and others ask how. People often assume they heard a booming voice or at least something that came from outside the person.

But any Christian who has a rapport with God can testify that something inside speaks. It's not your mind, because the Holy Spirit speaks faster than any thought you can have. It's quick, sharp and comes out of nowhere, so to speak.

The Holy Spirit teaches us from inside. The problem with hearing this still, small voice is that if I really want something, it's very easy to hear a yes. Having had the wrong spirit talk to me from inside for so many years, I know you can think a voice is God's when it isn't.

That's why seeking confirmation of a word is so important—especially if you really want something and you keep hearing yes. Ask any number of couples who married because they heard a yes, when it was really their emotions talking all along. Countless lives have been ruined because of a false sense of peace that masked the actual will of God.

If you really seek God, you will know when the still, small voice says yes from inside; the peace that passes no earthly understanding will accompany that voice. Then you know you are in God's will. You'll have no turmoil over your decision, and when hassles arise, you can recall your memory-makers, God's revelation to you.

A word of warning: Too many Christians have the impression that if a door opens they should walk through it. That's being a fatalist and can have grievous consequences. Say you're looking for a job, and there are openings at Hardee's, Burger King and Sears. The Hardee's offer is the best. Most people assume God would want you at Hardee's, because the offer is so good.

So you pick Hardee's, but God knows that the building is going to burn down and you'll be out of a job. You based your decision on circumstances, because you were looking out for your own future. Had you waited on God for the Sears job, you would have been in His will, maybe led someone to Jesus, or simply enjoyed the job!

> Yes, we all know God opens doors, but do yourself a favor—don't go through just because it's open. As Christians, we cannot be fatalists.

Casting Lots

To me, this is a lazy way of getting guidance and although God allowed the disciples to use it in choosing Judas's replacement, I know how unpredictable this method can be. One time, though, God used casting lots to overrule my selfishness and prompt me to obey.

I was at the YWAM base in Hawaii and about to leave for a trip overseas. Very clearly I heard the Lord tell me to give a hundred dollars to one of the island boys to help him with his airfare home. I hemmed and hawed and pushed away the word because I only had a hundred dollars for myself for a six-week trip. I finally took three strips of paper, wrote 25, 50 and 100 on them and rolled them into little balls. I tossed them in the air; the one I caught and opened would indicate the amount of money I would give to the islander. Of course, it was the paper with 100 on it. At the airport—with six dollars to my name—someone handed me a bon voyage card containing $125.

need to trust

Sortes Biblicae

That's the Latin name for a method of determining God's will that was used by the church in the Middle Ages. I call it Bible roulette, and God has spoken to me numerous times when I sought Him in this unhurried way. Using this method, you close your eyes, ask a question, open the Bible, point to a verse and open your eyes to read the verse you've selected.

But this method is frowned upon for the same reasons casting lots is. It's a sloppy way to get guidance, because if you don't like what you read, you can always do it again. I've been guilty of this myself; as a young Christian I used this method often, but as I grew older in the Lord He didn't speak to me this way as often. Like all things in God, He does move us on to more mature ways of knowing Him and hearing His voice.

Fleeces

This is a way of seeking confirmation. This too can be horribly abused, because if you don't like the outcome of your fleece, you can always try again the way Gideon did.

After some time in Tonga, I was invited to go on an outreach in Singapore. I prayed in my two thousand dollars and got my plane ticket. A week before I was to leave a call came in indicating that the outreach was cancelled. I began to cry; I so wanted off that island. As I opened my Bible, a tear fell right on a verse that read, "and Jesus had compassion on her and said don't cry" (Luke 7:13, NAS). I knew immediately that the verse meant I was to go even though there would be no outreach. The next day on the beach, I said, "God, if you really want me to go to Singapore, make some fish jump out of the sea."

All of a sudden, a school of fish came flying out at least six feet into the air. I'll never forget the rush I felt as I saw the water fall off the fish and back into the sparkling sea. I said, "Wow! Do it again!" Within minutes, I saw a repeat performance by another school of fish.

Now I had my memory-maker, and I was going to need it.

. When the plane landed in New Zealand, I was told by the airline that I was not booked on the flight to Singapore the next day, that the plane was full and that, in fact, it had been chartered. I had my word and went to the airport the next day anyway. I got on the flight with no problem, and to make a long story short, the trip led to a divine appointment months later with the king of Tonga.

As I'm sure you know, God has three answers to our prayer requests: yes, no and wait. I once had several thousand dollars to invest, and for a while I was making a lot of money off the stock I had bought. But then it began to plummet. I couldn't get a word about whether to sell it or not, so I did what seemed logical and sold it at a small loss. Days later the stock soared. I remember God telling me, "In the future, when you don't know what to do and you haven't got a yes or a no, don't do anything." That waiting is so hard for me.

Sermons . . . and Billboards

God also speaks through sermons, books and music. He said in His Word that if we would diligently seek Him we would find Him. But be ready for His answer to be different from what you wanted, and be prepared to obey.

Eph. 6:17 says, *"Take the . . . the sword of the Spirit, which is the word of God."* I was taught, as you probably were, that the sword is the Word of God. But the "w" is not capitalized. It's not referring to the Bible. I believe that once we have our personal word from God, then that's the sword we must use to fight for the thing God has told us to do. Remember this: The Lord leads, draws and prompts us into His will. The enemy, however, gives us direction that's impulsive, demanding, compelling and pushy. Don't be afraid to go to your Father for the answers to your questions, for those who seek Him will be found by Him.

173

Over the years I have been amazed by the wonderful ways that God has spoken to me. It is these conversations that make my relationship with Him what it is.

One year, on the way home from preaching a New Years' Eve service, I rushed out to start the three-hour drive home, hoping to arrive before the bars let out. By mistake, I turned onto the interstate heading in the wrong direction. That was bad enough, but then I realized it was nine miles to the next exit, my first opportunity to turn around. I was pretty annoyed.

As I beat myself up and panicked at the thought of all the drunks I'd have to deal with in a few hours, I glanced over at a billboard. I got a revelation—and had a good laugh. It read, "Don't Have a Cow!" I turned on the radio, listened to Dick Clark announcing the countdown to midnight and praised God for all He had done that year. Oddly enough, I hardly saw any traffic at all.

Twenty-Six

Overcoming Rejection

"But first he must suffer many things and be rejected
by this generation."
—Luke 17:25

As Christians, we are expected to identify with Christ's sufferings, though few of us find it comfortable. But like Christ, all of us have been rejected to some degree and for a variety of reasons. As a result, we carry around the emotional baggage of rejection wherever we go.

As Christians, we are also expected to comfort others with the same comfort with which God has comforted us, though too few of us are equipped to do so. We need to be healed ourselves; to have that happen, we need to unpack our baggage.

Because the fear of rejection controls so many people, the church has become crippled. We respond to

/sad

175

people based on that fear, and we respond to God in the same way when He doesn't answer our prayers or when He allows a crisis that throws us for a loop.

In my life I'd had so many disappointing relationships that when I became a Christian, it was inevitable that at some point I'd take it all out on God. Fortunately, I can look back now and see how I've changed. I don't respond to rejection the same way anymore, because of the confidence I have now in God's love for me.

Please don't rush through this chapter. Here you'll see how people in the Bible responded to rejection. You may still have bottled-up anger and resentment toward people who wounded you. Maybe, like me, you've been wounded by a spiritual giant; that kind of betrayal runs deep. But as we look at the following people we'll see which ones responded incorrectly and which ones grew as a result of injustice. Our goal should be to shed the bitterness and allow the circumstances to help us grow spiritually.

Jesus

Picture our Lord surrounded by a mocking crowd. His hands are tied behind His back. Even if He wanted to, He couldn't defend Himself. People are pushing, punching, pulling on His beard. He's blindfolded, completely at the mercy of His attackers. There's a punch to His stomach and someone yells, "Prophesy, who hit You?"

Now let's look at another scene. Jesus is a prisoner of the state. Pilate traditionally releases a criminal of the crowd's choosing at an annual festival. In front of the jeering group stand Jesus and Barabbas, a murderer.

Overwhelmingly, the crowd chooses to have Barabbas released. For Jesus, this meant certain crucifixion.

Here's one more situation involving Jesus. The Lord asks His disciples to watch and pray. He goes off to be alone in His agony, certain of the doom that awaits Him. After releasing His fate to the Father, Jesus returns to see His entrusted followers sound asleep. Those who had been with Him all along don't seem to care.

Of the three situations, I think this one hurt Jesus the most. The disciples had no idea what their lack of concern conveyed. These men weren't out to hurt Jesus, but they did. These were the very men with whom Jesus had shared His heart, His secrets and His love. They owed Him their allegiance, but at a crucial moment, they stung Him with their rejection.

The Ten Lepers

In Luke 17 we find the story of ten lepers. They're covered with scabby boils; the law states no one is to touch them. They are considered unclean, and to most people, cursed by God.

Imagine you're a leper coming to town to shop. On the way in, you hear people yelling, "Unclean coming through!" How would you feel as people steered clear of you or threw rocks at you or shouted, "Go away, you cursed thing!"

Obviously, God hates you, right? Your heart is full of poison, especially toward God. Now, imagine that Jesus heals you of this terrible disease, and you don't even thank Him. Well, that's exactly what happened in this story. When Jesus healed the ten lepers, only one returned to glorify God and fall at the Lord's feet in gratitude.

The others were no doubt simply too full of bitterness and hatred, all because of the rejection they had faced daily—not only from others but seemingly from God as well. Their hearts were simply too hard and their spirits too crushed to receive the love that came with that healing.

Friend, don't let anything cause your heart to harden even for an hour. It's more dangerous than you can imagine. If you're in that situation now, read on and see what other strongholds surface. Be prepared for God's dealing—and His healing.

Abraham and Lot

Genesis 13 tells us about the parting of Abraham and his nephew Lot. As we saw before, the two families had outgrown the land, and Lot was allowed to choose which parcel of land he wanted for himself. He chose the more lucrative land, possibly, as many think, because he was selfish and greedy. But what if he was motivated by fear? He may have been feeling scared and rejected. After all, Abraham wasn't just his uncle. He was his friend and his mentor. They had been through "a lot" together, and now Abraham is leaving him. Lot is coming out from under his spiritual covering. It's time to grow up, and that's a scary thing for anyone. No wonder he chose the better land.

But Lot was in for a rude awakening. He was about to face tremendous rejection in this place where he has chosen to live. The people of Sodom called him "alien." They resented having this godly man walking around, telling them to repent from their wicked ways. God sent angels to warn Lot to leave before God destroyed the evil town. The perverts of Sodom wanted to rape Lot's guests, the angels, but Lot offered his virgin daughters instead.

What a strange thing for a father to do. Now I'm not out to make a doctrine of this, but let's assume for a minute that Lot is simply starved for some interaction with holiness. After all, he had little or no affirmation of his righteous behavior. What if he reacted out of starvation for fellowship? Could it be his own walk with God had been tested so much he was also becoming hardened?

The angels tell him he must leave the city, but Lot hesitates. To me, that shows something was wrong with his walk. He should have simply been obedient. He argues about where the angels are telling him to go; then his sons-in-law mock him and refuse to go.

His wife disobeyed, looked back and became a brick. After he reached the town where he wanted to go, he ended up moving to a cave. He has only his two daughters with him; he has lost nearly all of his descendants. Two nights in a row his daughters got him drunk and slept with him, hoping to get pregnant.

How do you think Lot felt when he looked back on all that had happened to him?

 Our comfort and healing can come only when we keep our eyes on God and allow Him to bring peace to our spirit. If we pull away in the slightest from our devotion to God, then we will certainly end up turning to something else for comfort.

Joseph

Genesis 37 begins to recount the ordeal of Joseph, who suffered major rejection when his brothers dropped him in a pit and left him there to die while they went off to have dinner. Then the brothers sell Joseph to a passing caravan for twenty pieces of silver.

Joseph reaches Egypt and is bought by Potiphar, an officer of pharaoh and a very important man. Somehow, Joseph kept a good attitude through all this and as a result, Potiphar was blessed. For a while, Joseph was treated well and given significant responsibility.

Then the next injustice comes. Potiphar's wife claims he tried to rape her, and Joseph is jailed. He stays close to God and is blessed. After a while he interprets a dream, and when his interpretation comes to pass, he asks the beneficiary of his interpretation, the king's cupbearer, to remind the king that Joseph is still imprisoned. Two years go by before the cupbearer remembers—and that's only because Pharaoh wants someone to interpret a bad dream he had.

Joseph continued to make the best of the cage he was in and eventually, in God's perfect timing, Joseph was elevated to do God's purpose, preserving his own family and nation during a severe famine.

Joseph's response to his brothers was this: "You meant it for evil, but God meant it for good" (Gen. 50:20, NAS). How many of us can say that to those who have wronged us?

Right now, you may feel boxed in. Remember, you don't know the future, and you don't know the activity of God behind the scenes. Can you accept your situation and forgive those you need to forgive? Can you ask God to forgive you for the sins in your heart, because you've reacted in the flesh to your jail? Go on, you can do it. It will free God to elevate you to a new plateau. Do like Joseph did. He rose to the occasion no matter what situation he was in.

180

Leah

The story of Jacob finding a wife begins in Genesis 29. When Jacob first meets two sisters, Rachel and Leah, he falls for Rachel. Rachel was beautiful; Leah had weak eyes, whatever that means. Jacob rejected Leah right off the bat, even though as the older sister she was to be married first. Laban tricks Jacob into marrying Leah instead of Rachel; how that happened is a story in itself.

Anyway, in the morning Jacob finds Leah lying next to him and yells at his new father-in-law for deceiving him. Can you imagine how Leah felt? She gave herself to Jacob, and now he's totally disgusted. Jacob is stuck with her. A week later, he marries Rachel and loves her more than Leah. Can you imagine a lifetime of knowing that your husband didn't want you in the first place? What rejection and humiliation she must have felt. She had to live with continual blows to her spirit. But she, too, rose to the occasion. She drew closer to God, as evidenced by the names she gave her many children.

Tamar

This young daughter of King David is raped by her half-brother. She is now barren and unclean, defiled for life. No one will want her. She goes to live with her other brother and withdraws from the world. Her relationship with God is unclear, but I'm sure at some point she cried, *Why me?*

Rape, incest and molestation of any kind are horrible offenses that can damage a person forever. The resulting shame, guilt, self-rejection, hatred and bitterness can eat you up so you end up barren and withdrawn yourself.

yes they can as it did me

181

If you've been assaulted, abused or raped, don't blame yourself, and don't let anyone else blame you. Forgive the offender and press on through your emotions. Remember, you're a new creature in Christ. Forget the past and move on. Please don't end up like Tamar—introverted, barren, emotionally cut off from future relationships.

Peter

Now let's look again at Peter. As a new convert, he wanted to be the best disciple he could be. But Jesus rebuked Peter in front of a crowd, and I would guess he was a bit humiliated. In his zeal, Peter cuts the ear off a guard, and Jesus puts the ear back on, embarrassing him further.

Later, Peter is walking at a distance, probably feeling a bit dejected, when someone asks if he knows Jesus. Peter angrily denies it.

What Peter has just done is deny his spiritual leader. Spiritual leaders are placed over us for a reason, to guard our souls. What can we learn from Peter's reaction? If you feel that your pastor or other church leader has rejected you, go to the one you're estranged from and talk it out. Don't overreact and leave the church. I've heard countless stories from people who left a church because they thought the pastor didn't like them.

From the moment we receive Christ and become His children, He begins cleaning us up. Most of us got rid of the big ugly sins right away. But then we faced years of surgery to remove the next layer. Finally, we have to deal with all the little sins that are ingrained in us, the ones that have rolled in over the years to take the place of hope and joy, love and trust, confidence and peace—and those, my friend, may take a lifetime to purge.

The Prophets

The prophets weren't without their own rejections. Jeremiah, who had a direct call and mandate from God, endured much rejection. His job was to publicly denounce the sins of the people—and the leaders. Jeremiah was a sympathetic and sensitive man by nature. He faced so much opposition and the pain was so deep in his heart that more than once he wanted to throw in the towel.

Elijah, too, felt rejected by God because the people wouldn't believe what he had to say. He knew the people were cursing him.

Hosea had it pretty bad himself. He was married to a woman who continually played the harlot, and yet Hosea was required by God to accept and love her.

Malachi was hated by the entire land because he rebuked the people for their neglect in worshipping the true God.

Although they suffered much disapproval, resentment and disdain, these men of God left an example—that no matter what people do or say about us, we are commanded to love and to fulfill God's will moment by moment, whether we like it or not.

Demas

He's mentioned only twice in the New Testament. We first see his name as one of the inner circle. He was respected and apparently one of the boys. But the next time we hear of him, Paul tells Timothy that Demas has left him because he loved the world more.

Why do I bring his name up here? You will have friends in the church who seem to be moving with the vision but suddenly aren't there anymore. You've lost a friend, a colleague, a brother in the faith, because they dropped out of the race. Don't judge them or take their withdrawal personally. It would be easy to feel they've rejected you, but like Paul, you must keep your eyes fixed on the mission ahead of you. It could be that they just got weary and needed someone to help them be restored.

Twenty-Seven

Needing a Reprieve

*"But thanks be to God that, though you used to be
slaves to sin, you wholeheartedly obeyed the form of
teaching to which you were entrusted. You have been
set free from sin and have become slaves to
righteousness."*
—Romans 6:17-18

Let's look at an obvious question: How much can
Satan do in the life of a believer?

If Satan caused Ananias to lie, Judas to betray and
prophets to give false predictions (see 2 Chron. 18:18-
21), then we have proof that spirits of "the evil one"
can cause us to sin.

In John 14:30 Jesus said, "The prince of this world
is coming. He has no hold on me." That is the key. We
must not allow an open door for the enemy. Hebrews
4:15 reminds us that Jesus was tempted in all the ways
we are "yet was without sin." He listened and did what
His Father told Him. As a result, He didn't sin.

Let me tell you about an unbeliever named Larry. A generally mild-mannered man, Larry resented the job he felt he was stuck with and seemed to lose his temper only at work. He never expressed his anger in loud outbursts, but inside he stewed a little. The bumper-to-bumper commute each morning would quickly obliterate any good mood he might have started the day with. By the time his car pulled into the parking lot, Larry was late for work and poisoned with animosity.

A tiny, dark spot on his heart so far was evident only in the spiritual realm, but the evil—in Larry's case, the resentment—that stems from the heart was activated. Once in the office, all he wanted was a hot cup of coffee, but as usual, Larry's lazy, self-centered colleagues had left the pot empty. Now Larry was really mad.

Self had become the dominating factor in his emotions. *I was inconvenienced by that horrible traffic. I just wanted some hot coffee. Is that too much to ask? I have an important job here. Why didn't they make a fresh pot so I could have some?*

Larry stomped into his office only to discover that his secretary had been taken ill and did not finish the presentation he needed that morning. He now has someone specific to be mad at, and his mind churns with all the possible ways he should handle her incompetence.

As he entertains these vicious thoughts, more darkness appears on his heart. The evil one knows it's there, and if he can make Larry's heart just a little bit blacker, Larry won't be able to control himself. The darkness grows as he envisions himself yelling at his secretary and firing her—although what he'd really like to do is slap her.

So far, Larry's anger has existed only in his mind and emotions. But his will is about to come into play. He will make a conscious and irrational decision to manifest evil behavior because so far, he's having one evil day (see Eph. 6:13).

Larry is still fuming when his boss comes in. With a raised voice clearly intended to humiliate him, Mr. Boss bellows, "You're late almost every day. Your presentation isn't done because you procrastinate— don't try to blame your secretary! Empty your desk. You're fired." The self raises up inside and sends powerful signals to his anger.

Larry loses his temper and hits his desk (it was closer than the roof). In the process, he knocks over a photo of his precious wife and children, which shatters on the floor. Now, with all the darkness and defilement emanating from his blackened heart, Larry does something very unlike himself.

He eyes the computer. A thought flashes through his mind: *They'll be lost without the information I've got stored in there.* He picks up the computer and throws it out the window, knowing the devastation this will bring to his boss and to the company. An hour later Larry is in jail for destruction of personal property.

Now let's try a different scenario. Larry arrives at the office in a bad mood after a nerve-racking commute. But this time, a Christian intervenes. She sees the empty coffee pot and the look on Larry's face. "Hey, I'll make a fresh pot. You go on to your office. I'll bring you a cup when it's finished brewing," she says. A few minutes later, as she sets the mug down on his desk, she adds, "Let me know if there's anything I can do for you today. I heard Barbara's out sick."

This time when the boss enters Larry's office, he finds a much different man from the one in the previous scenario. "I know you want that paper now, and Carol has offered to help with the presentation," Larry says. "It will be done in time for the meeting."

Mr. Boss's annoyance at Larry has just been defused. He decides to give him another chance and invites him to lunch.

Carol's intervention has helped lead Larry away from the temptation to explode in anger. More importantly, simply through her calming presence she delivered Larry from the angry state he was in. His snowballing sin was diverted, and his evil day didn't end with the evil one holding him captive to do more wrong.

This is precisely what Jesus does for us. He is our Carol, our coffee girl, the calming presence in our frenetic, stress-filled lives. When we choose to ignore Him, our actions are no different from what Larry's would have been had he had knocked the coffee mug out of the Carol's hand and said, "Forget it!"

If you're not familiar with the first recorded outburst of anger in the Bible, read Gen. 4:4-16 to familiarize yourself with Cain's situation. As the account goes, God rejected Cain's offering but accepted Abel's. Whether Cain's main problem was rejection, jealousy or pride is anyone's guess. But Gen. 4:5 says that Cain "was very angry, and his face was downcast." In other words, he's ticked off, and it shows.

God says to him, "Why are you angry? Why is your face downcast? If you do what is right, will you not be accepted? But if you do not do what is right, sin is crouching at your door; it desires to have you, but you must master it." If you choose to pout or continue in

188

anger, He says, you will open the door to more things that will anger you, and you will be uncontrollably mad and unhappy. This is a given.

But He tells Cain that he could stop that cycle right then as well as in the future, by mastering righteous reactions rather than evil ones. The evil one and his nature are always at your door waiting to come and master you.

Prov. 16:6 tells us that "through the fear of the LORD a man avoids evil." Had Cain known that fear, he would have chosen God and His life and His way. He had the chance to walk in the light. Instead, he chose evil and its nature, and its destructive nature separated him from God. He let darkness have mastery over him. He made the decision to murder his brother and followed through with it—just like Larry, who decided to take revenge on his boss and throw the computer out the window. Don't laugh—sin is sin, right?

Like Larry, Cain ends up in a prison of his own making. Only far worse for Cain, he is banished from the presence of God because he did not choose Him when the choice was clearly placed before him. In 1 John 3:12 believers are warned not to be like Cain, "who belonged to the evil one." What a terrible legacy.

Both Larry and Cain listened to the wrong temptation. Cain was given a second chance, a reprieve, a cup of coffee so to speak—a moment in which love and truth were offered. He could have chosen at that moment not to go any further with the evil one. He could have walked with God. Larry, on the other hand, needed a second chance. He needed to hear a voice of peace, goodness and deliverance—just as we all do.

Twenty-Eight

Ambassadors of Reconciliation

*"He has committed to us the message
of reconciliation. We are therefore
Christ's ambassadors."*
—*2 Corinthians 5:19-20*

". . . Jesus sends greetings. He is always wrestling in prayer for you, that you may stand firm in all the will of God, mature and fully assured."

What? Jesus sends greetings? Jesus is wrestling in prayer for me? Where's that in the Bible?

It's not. As any Bible scholar will tell you, the above verse is a perfect example of taking scripture out of context. Not only have I done that, but also I didn't even give the complete verse. But because God can and does use anything to get our attention, let me slide on this for a while, OK?

I read that verse segment one day when I was opening the Bible to Philippians but overshot it and ended up in the fourth chapter of Colossians. There, at the beginning of the page, was the portion of verse 12 that I've quoted above. It pierced my heart with such love that tears came to my eyes. (In case you're wondering, verse 12 starts out "Epaphras, who is one of you and a servant of Christ Jesus, sends greetings . . ." but somehow it changed for me.)

How comforting it was to know that sometimes Jesus says *Hi.* It's like a phone call from an old friend. Here it was as if Jesus Himself was saying, *"Chris, you don't do such a great job praying for yourself, and you've got a lot of spiritual warfare going on. So my dear, I'm doing battle for you so you will not get knocked out of the ring and miss your destiny."*

The crux of what I had to relearn during the time I lost heart was that it is God's will in my life that matters. Jesus had given His life, and I was to give mine even if that meant certain of my desires had to die. I also had to understand that just because I was saved and willing to lay down my life for the kingdom, that didn't mean I wasn't going to get knocked around by the powers of hell. And, oddly enough, this would eventually strengthen me!

Peter was a person much like you or me. Jesus warns him that "Satan has asked to sift you as wheat" (Luke 22:31). Any good thesaurus will give you a host of synonyms for the word sift: analyze, clean, drain, examine, explore, investigate, purify, screen, scrutinize, search, separate and strain, among others.

I had always been under the impression that when Satan sifted Peter, it was simply to give him a hard time, to thwart the purposes of God. But it's the sifting of wheat that purifies it. Actually, Satan does us a favor

STUDY

by sifting us! As Satan examines our reactions, we get to see what's in our hearts.

#truth

Then, in the very next verse of Luke 22, Jesus gives a prophetic word and a directive to His disciple: "But I have prayed for you, Simon, that your faith may not fail. And when you have turned back, strengthen your brothers."

Peter, though, didn't catch the implication, and went on to declare: "Lord, I am ready to go with you to prison and to death" (verse 33).

We all start out in our walk with the Lord with the best of intentions—hopeful, energetic to see how God will use us and answer our prayers—but the sins, failures and hurts we incur along the way change us. Jesus keeps praying for us as He promised He would do, but unfortunately, we can simply become numb and hinder the guidance and promptings of God as He attempts to do His work through us.

true

It's interesting to note that in verse 32, Jesus called Peter by his former name, Simon, when He warned him about the sifting to come. But He called him Peter, his new name, when he tells Peter that he will deny Him three times before the rooster crows.

In Jesus' choice of names I see the contrast between Peter's new name and his old nature. In effect, Jesus is saying, *"Simon, even though you have a new nature and a new name, as a follower of Mine you will blow it. You will resort back to old ways. But after you realize it and remember that I am on your side, don't be ashamed that you gave up and withdrew. Use what you have learned to strengthen others: Feed my sheep."*

Earlier, Jesus had told His disciples, "If you love me, you will obey what I command" (John 14:15). Like

193

Peter, we can say we love the Lord but we treat Him the way we treated our parents: We loved them, but we still disobeyed. We still inched our way around them, trying to figure out just how far we could push them, how much we could get away with without getting caught.

The love relationship we have with Jesus isn't based on what we do for Him and His kingdom. That's pretty basic, but it's still a lesson we all have to learn and sometimes, relearn. But I am convinced that the abundant life He promises us comes as a result of our obedient response to those promptings of His Spirit to become fishers of men—those "men" being both unbelievers and believers who have blown it.

"For we are God's workmanship, created in Christ Jesus to do good works, which God prepared in advance for us to do" (Eph. 2:10). With all my running away, God never let go of the call He has for me, and He won't do any less for you.

In Matthew 21 Jesus tells the parable of a man who asked his two sons to work in the vineyard for him. One son said, "I will, sir" but did not go; the other son "I will not" but later he changed his mind and went.

Which one of the two do you resemble when it comes to working in God's vineyard and sowing seed for Him, no matter how much you may get banged up in the process? Maybe as a new believer, in your zeal and desire to reach others for Christ, you made a mental decision that you would always witness for the Lord no matter where He might send you—Africa, Asia or just around the corner.

Maybe you did obey the promptings and gave the Spirit of God opportunities to minister to others through you. Like the rest of us, you were amazed at the results and the way He brought it all about. But now, when the Holy Spirit tells you to jump, you ask, "Why?" The hurts that have piled up over the years have hardened you. You still sing songs that express your willingness to have God use you, and you still respond to altar calls to prove you're ready again to go into battle. But the problem is, you don't go, and you don't finance those who *do* go. So you say, "Yes," but through your actions your, "Yes," has turned into a "No."

But maybe you're like the other son. You said you wouldn't go because you felt so unworthy or so inadequate. You sat back and heard the stories of the divine encounters your friends have had, and now you are ready to go out and touch others, no matter what kind of hurt or hardship comes your way. That's great! I hope you will be encouraged to follow the promptings of the obedient side to your spirit.

When it comes to having a ministry most people will never hold a microphone, stand behind the pulpit or witness before a large group. Most likely, God will do with you what He did with the demoniac. The Lord delivered him, healed him and made him whole, and although the man wanted to work in the ministry alongside Jesus, the Lord sent him home to testify. God wanted him to reach a certain group of people with his story of deliverance. Quite possibly, that meant only his family or the people he met in his everyday life. The Lord sent him back to a specific area for a specific purpose.

It can be a scary thing to witness to others, especially if you have a more reserved personality. But when it comes to witnessing for the Lord, there's a dynamic at work that you won't find anywhere else: When you open your mouth, God's Spirit breathes on the very words you speak. No matter what you say, if it is kingdom-minded, it is kingdom-sent. There is life behind your words, regardless of how simple they may sound to you. "The word goes forth with power" isn't just a nice phrase; it's the truth!

One morning, I spoke at an elementary school and was asked how I met the Lord. It was a challenge in itself just to share to a group that age, but as they sat down before me, I realized how carefully I had to choose my words. Most testimonies emphasize the "before" aspect to show what the person was delivered from. But I also wanted to show the way God drew me in even when I was oblivious to His activity. A few moments into my sermonette, all the kids stopped fidgeting and seemed entranced. Their little eyes had gotten as big as saucers. But they weren't looking at me. They were staring over my head toward the skylight behind me.

A minute later they were motionless, looking straight at me. Once I finished and the teacher dismissed the children, a few lined up to talk to me. I always try to speak privately to people so that no one else can hear what they're saying to me. One by one I called them over. Much to my surprise, they all had a similar story to tell me: *While you were talking, Jesus was looking through the window.*

I believe that what they saw is the evidence of what happens in the spiritual realm when we give our testimony or preach His word. The Lord stands there, watching over His word to perform it. He breathes life and power into it. So be encouraged: All you have to do is open your mouth and because you are an ambassador of Christ, He will anoint what you say in order to reconcile people to Himself.

Many of you are familiar with the story in Luke 14 about the man who planned to hold a big dinner party. He sent his slave out to gather up those who had been invited. But they all made excuses. Guest No. 1 said he had bought a piece of land and wanted to go look at it. No. 2 said he had bought five yoke of oxen and wanted to go try them out. No. 3 simply used the excuse that he was married.

This parable is usually used in reference to a wonderful invitation to come to Christ for salvation. But I'd like to show a different interpretation of this dinner invitation story. I believe it offers a timeless warning that followers of Christ will find all sorts of excuses not to do the work of the kingdom, and God exhorts us with these few words: "What good is it if a man claims to have faith but has no deeds?" (James 2:14).

The invited guests were indifferent to their host; their excuses for not attending are not that different from the excuses we give for not working in the Father's vineyard. *Let someone else do it; I'm busy.*

Guest No. 1 used land as an excuse. That's the equivalent of the material things that occupy our time and divert our money away from the vineyard. Whether it's watching TV, participating in sports, puttering around the garden, spiffing up the car or going out to a movie, so many things consume the little free time we seem to have. Guest No. 1 may have worked hard to acquire the things in his life, and he intended to enjoy them.

Guest No. 2 places priority on his oxen—his business investment. Many of us have been forced to work long hours simply to make a living. That's unfortunate, but if God is responsible to supply all our needs, then we should work in His vineyard when He asks us to. Others are so consumed by their work—and not always out of necessity—that they feel they have no time for the Lord's work.

Guest No. 3 blames his absence on his wife. I shouldn't have to repeat this, but I will: Don't let other people hinder you from keeping God's divine appointments. If He already planned those appointments for the time when you would be in Christ Jesus, then certainly He planned them around your possessive, self-centered, insecure relatives!

Fortunately, unlike the host who excludes these three guests from ever being invited again, God continues to urge you "to reaffirm your love for him" (2 Cor. 2:8). That means you must put kingdom interests over your own and do the next thing He tells you to do.

God will give you plenty of opportunities to show that you love Him. He'll prompt *you* to give food and drink to those in need. He'll lead *you* to visit the sick or help those in prison—two groups in particular that are ripe for harvest. He will lead *you* to clean out your closet and give your clothing to the less fortunate. For as you do these things, you do them unto Him.

Twenty-Nine

Painless Witnessing

*"Take the talent from him and give it to the one
who has the ten talents."*
—Matthew 25:28

Jesus expects us to use the gifts and talents He
bestows on us to lead others to Him and increase His
family on earth. He has also told us to make disciples
of all the nations. So now I'm in a dilemma. Do I go
fishing for men, or do I concentrate my energy on
equipping the saints? Is my ministry outside the church
or inside it?

One would think that there would be far less chance
of facing rejection or ostracism if we concentrated our
efforts within the four walls of the church, pouring out
our lives for our spiritual brethren. But you and I know
that's not the case. Even so, as we have little by little
lost our zeal for soul-winning because of the hurts in
our lives, the church has become our retreat. If I have

to do something for God, let me do it there. Somehow it at least seems safer.

The deception here lies in the assumption that as long as I'm in the church, I'm serving God. The church becomes for us part hospital and part workplace — but all too soon we realize that there's only so much room in the clinic and only so many jobs to be filled in this "workplace." In short, there are only so many people allowed in the church's "in-group."

Many pastors I've met are baffled by the number of visitors that come a few times and never return. They want to know what it is that's sending them away. I'd venture to say that the answer isn't a *what*; it's a *who.*

Maybe you can remember a time in your childhood when a new kid came to school and started hanging out with you and your best friend. The next thing you knew, the new kid was with your best friend exclusively. You had been ousted, or maybe your best friend found a romantic interest and then had no time for you.

A similar situation can happen in church. Those who have gravitated toward the pastor and the church leadership soon begin to see this inner circle as their private in-group. To them, the church has become something of an exclusive country club, and they are wary of new people coming in and usurping their position in ministry, or stealing the affections of the in-group. They may have gained strength and confidence through their purpose and identity at the church, and they simply want to keep things they way they are. When new people come in, they become territorial. Visitors who come seeking a place where they can be healed of their own hurts often discover an invisible barricade shielding them from the pastor and the leaders—and from any possibility of genuine help.

The same type of insecurity existed among the disciples, those people who were closest to Jesus and should have been the most secure people on earth at the time. But they even pushed away people who wanted to get close to Jesus. In Luke 18:15, we see that people were bringing their babies to Jesus so they could be touched by the Son of God. What did the disciples do? "When the disciples saw this, they rebuked them" (verse 15). Of course, the Lord in turn rebuked the disciples!

Later in the same chapter, we see a blind beggar calling to Jesus: "Jesus, Son of David, have mercy on me!" (verse 38). Then we're told that "those who led the way"—no doubt, the disciples again—"rebuked him and told him to be quiet" (verse 39). In our day, they'd be more likely to say, *"Shut up! He can't be bothered with the likes of you!"* Finally, they see Zacchaeus, a wealthy tax collector. Tax collectors were about as much respected in those days as lawyers are today; they were considered to be bottom-feeders at best. Because Zacchaeus was short, he had climbed a tree to get a better look at Jesus. Now Jesus—who should know better than to have anything do with such low-life— actually calls the man by name: "Zacchaeus, come down immediately. I must stay at your house today" (Luke 19:5). So the man clambers down the tree "and welcomed him gladly" (verse 6). But what does the in crowd do now? "All the people saw this and began to mutter, 'He has gone to be the guest of a sinner'" (verse 7).

Why weren't the disciples full of joy that so many wanted to be near the Lord, near them, near the action? Because they didn't want to risk their place next to the leader. This same desire, this need for some kind of a pecking order, surfaces in Matthew 20 with the mother of the sons of Zebedee. "Grant that one of these two sons of mine may sit at your right and the other at your left in your kingdom," she requests in verse 21. "You don't know what you are asking," Jesus responded (verse 22). E-ee-k—wrong request!

So many Christians have been chewed up pretty badly by the world or by those around them in their everyday lives, the church has become their safe haven. It becomes *my* club with members *I* want to be associated with. After all, if we get a bunch of sinners coming in, what does that make me? Let's just keep things the way they have always been—our church, our club, our ministry.

But if "the steps of a man are established by the Lord" (Ps. 37:23, NAS), then the righteous must not keep others from any opportunity to meet the Lord and fellowship with Him and His people. Many times when I was ready to run, quit or jump the gun, God guided my steps into my destiny or simply affirmed His will in my life. How can we possibly presume He would do any less when it comes to drawing people to Himself? God goes to great lengths to place us, with split-second timing, next to someone He's working on. We have to provide an open door, not another barricade.

In New York, there is a grandmother who is up at the crack of dawn, tiptoeing through the house to a quiet corner. On her knees she intercedes on behalf of her runaway granddaughter, believed to be somewhere in the Miami area. Her specific request this morning is for God to send a Christian her way.

Now you live in Miami, and you say a quick prayer as you rush out the door: "God, please use me today." When you get to your car, it won't start. You start griping at God, *"Why me?"* In a panic, you run down the street and hop the bus. As you get closer to the city, a group of teens stomp onto the bus and saunter right toward you with menacing looks and a few curse words spewing out intended to underscore their rebellious presence.

The most horrid-looking girl in the group sits next to you. You move away a bit in case she is contagious. The bus stops and her friends get off, leaving her behind. Here's your chance to make conversation, *"Don't you want to get off, too?"* you might ask. But you don't say a word. After all, you have your own problems to deal with today, what with a broken-down car and being forced to ride this crummy bus.

What you don't know is that this girl is a runaway, and her grandmother in New York has spent hours on her knees in prayer for this child. The girl isn't enjoying her so-called "freedom" anymore, but she's too scared to call home. God knew you were the perfect person to minister to her that day, not because you know the Bible, but because you know Jesus. But the real reason God chose you to help her is that because at one time, in your former life, you knew what it was like to be rebellious, scared and alone. You too had run away from home, but you've become so blinded by the cares of the world that you can't even recognize a mirror image of your former self when you see one.

Friends, it isn't just preaching that we are to do, it's offering a word in season, a word that comes from our experiences and our understanding, a word that brings healing and life. I can assure you of this, God knows exactly who to send to whom. So the next time your car won't start, praise God for the divine appointment He's going to send your way.

Danny Lehman, an old friend of mine from YWAM gave a teaching on evangelism that I've never forgotten.

Mark 4:28-29 says that "all by itself the soil produces grain—first the stalk, then the head, then the full kernel in the head. As soon as the grain is ripe, he puts the sickle to it, because the harvest has come."

Danny's insight into this is certain to demolish any feelings of inadequacy you may have about yourself when it comes to leading another person to Jesus. In order to grow a stalk of corn, the first thing you must do is loosen the soil by turning it over before you ever plant the seed. In the same way, people must be prepared to have the seed of the Word of God planted in their hearts. Some people you will meet are in no way ready to have the seed planted. Like uncultivated earth, they are so hard that they aren't ready to receive anything from you. Because of the hurts in their lives, these people are skeptical and cynical about your efforts to "save" them. There are a "gazillion" reasons why people have become so hardened, and getting them to make an about-face in their thinking is highly unlikely.

Then there are people in whom the seed has been planted, but the little nourishment they gave it resulted in little more than a spindly blade. They have chosen to say, "No" to the kingdom way of living and to God's only plan for salvation. It doesn't matter how nice you are when sharing the truth with people like this, because in effect what you're doing is calling this person uninformed, misdirected, brainwashed or, worst of all to their egos—wrong! So don't be surprised that people want to defend the form of "religion" they've settled on. By telling them something different, you're telling them that what they believe will send them to hell, and all that they base their life on is wrong.

Continuing in the growth cycle of a stalk of corn, the next element to appear is the head. This represents people who have had some religious teaching and now something has happened to make them ready for more. The mature grain appears, but it still isn't ripe for picking. You can challenge them to make a decision for God and leave it to the Holy Spirit to follow through or bring more watering into that person's life by some other way.

Fortunately, there are times when you'll meet people who have been so well-prepared and ready to meet God that you won't have to say much at all, because the hardest work has already been done. So pull out your holy hatchet and harvest them.

Friend, don't let anyone pressure you and deceive you into believing that you have to lead everyone you meet to Christ. Be like a gardener and discern where they are, how much water is too much, how much fertilizer is needed, and then commit them to the vinedresser to complete what He started. You can do more harm than good by trying to harvest dirt, a blade or even a head.

Finally, when you have a burden for a lost soul, remember that God does not want any to perish. He loves that person more than you do. He also has set eternity in the heart of man. Most people deep inside are inclined toward believing in a higher power and want a beautiful place to go to when they die. After all, don't most people assume they are going to heaven anyway? Take the striving out of evangelism. In John 6:44, Jesus says, *"No one can come to me unless the Father who sent me draws him."* God chooses, we introduce.

I would imagine many of you started out with all the fire and zeal most converts do, and you experienced the awe and thrill of seeing God's hand in your early witnessing. I have wonderful memories of seeing people go from hard dirt to a blade, from a head to a mature grain. Like many of you, I have witnessing stories I share over and over again. One that I cherish is the story of a woman who wrote to me about a prayer I prayed for her. She and her husband couldn't have children and had tried for several years to adopt. Within a month of our time together, she was given twin girls. You and I both know God brought those girls, not me. But the marvelous wonder at the part I played fuels me for more divine appointments.

The way Jesus repeatedly questioned Peter's love for Him is no different from the way He questions us. Do you really love Me? Then feed My sheep. But as we grow weary and deadened, the only love we can share is God's love, and if we fall out of faith and hope in Him, we have nothing to give to the sheep—or to the goats, for that matter.

In the end, though, because people are the way they are, regardless of how they got that way, God gives us His love for them. We certainly don't have the right kind of love to give, or at the very least we don't have enough of it. But we have to be on guard all the time, because if we're not careful, the world around us will help snuff out our love for the brethren, for our unsaved love ones and finally for God Himself. And we end up bankrupt in the love department (see Matt. 24:10-12).

Countless Christians out there are deeply grieved and are waiting for someone to come along who will not judge them but who will show them mercy and compassion on them. Too often, judgmental people come along and add more quicksand to the life of the one who's sinking.

By contrast, look at the way Jesus treats the woman at the well in John 4. He doesn't hammer on her about what a sinner she is. He lets her know He's aware of her promiscuous past, and that gets her attention. Then He offers her hope and before long, she runs into town, testifying about the Lord. Many believers who had sordid lifestyles before they were saved can bring hope to people who see no way out of the sinful and dark circumstances in which they're living.

You may be the one person God can use best to share His light with another specific individual. You can testify how your life was transformed, how you were saved and loved into the kingdom. Share about your prayers that were answered, your attitudes that were changed, the memory-makers you experienced, even the bumpy ride along the way. Yes, you may even need to share where you went wrong after you were saved and how God graciously protected and forgave you. God has said, *"Never will I leave you; never will I forsake you"* (Heb. 13:5), and that's a promise some brethren need to be reminded of.

Those of us who have been rescued after leaving the Father's home have a great testimony to share. We have the words that give renewed hope, because in our rebellion and hard-heartedness, in our tears and self-pity, Jesus never left us. He sent greetings to us in various ways. He tugged on our hearts to assure us we still belonged to Him.

He led us in the wilderness, that we might know what was in our hearts—not to condemn us but to change us. If you are like me, one day you came to your senses and realized it was time to call out to the Father. Now you can go share your story with the faint-hearted, the wounded saints.

If you've *meshubahed* even a little from the Father and are ready to return, don't be ashamed. Others, myself included, have had to re-choose to serve the living God and to endure disappointment in doing His will. My friend, don't delay. Call out these words to Father God and watch what happens: *"Restore to me the joy of your salvation and grant me a willing spirit, to sustain me. Then I will teach transgressors your ways, and sinners will turn back to you"* (Ps. 51:12-13).

As I lost my first love for Jesus, I found I couldn't care for others anymore. Doing for the kingdom was replaced by doing for Chris. But once I found my way back—and I can assure you, I did—my compassion had matured.

Recently, at an altar call, a woman stood before me with cold, stony eyes and admitted she was mad at God. Her husband had left and taken the kids; she said she was numb and couldn't sense God's presence any more.

A few years earlier I probably would have given her a pat answer, a Christian cliché, but now my eyes filled with tears because I knew exactly how she felt. I also saw the desperation on her face; it was as if she was asking, *"Will I ever feel close to God again?"* Im try

I told her that if I could come back, she could too. God would do something so wonderful that she wouldn't be able to keep her heart hard. I was able to give her hope, because I had come back, fully restored and in love with the Lord in a new way.

So how did I come back, you ask? Let me tell you.

Thirty

The Road Home

*"My disgrace is before me all day long, and my face
is covered with shame."*
—Psalm 44:15 *I feel this*

It was obvious to me that Satan was holding me
captive to do his will. As long as my heart was hard,
guilt would cripple me. Rom. 8:1 says, "Therefore, there
is now no condemnation for those who are in Christ
Jesus," and 1 John 3:21 says, "If our hearts do not
condemn us, we have confidence before God." Why
couldn't I believe that?

There's a huge difference between feeling utterly
condemned, which comes from Satan, and sensing the
conviction of the Holy Spirit. When we feel condemned,
we have no confidence in our standing with Him. The
sin in your life as a believer—and the resulting inability
to have a clear conscience—will shipwreck your faith.
But glory to God, He gives grace to those who humble

themselves and admit their sin. Jacob had to admit he was a deceiver and cheat; and Isaiah had to admit to being a man of unclean lips. <u>I had to admit I was backslidden.</u> me for sure

I vividly remember one day when I was driving to my mother's house several hours away. I could hardly see the road for the tears. I cried out loud, "Will I ever come back?" Instantly, into my spirit, came the answer: *Yes, you will.* At that point, it didn't matter when, or how, or where, as long as I knew I would come back. My biggest fear had been that in the twinkling of an eye I would die in rebellion to God and the work He had given me to do. That is an extremely heavy burden to carry around each day.

My cry was the same as Paul's. Whenever he was doing something that he knew he shouldn't be doing, he realized it would cause death and that Jesus Christ was the only one who could deliver him (see Rom. 7:15-25). My conversion had been so easy. Would God do it again? Could I go from a hard heart to a soft one? How much would I have to change to get into His good graces? How much had I messed up my destiny?

A verse came to my mind that day: "I would have despaired unless I believed that I would see the goodness of the Lord in the land of the living" (Ps. 27:13, NAS). I had my memory-makers; I knew what God had done for me. I had known His sweet presence. I had partaken of His heavenly nature and had seen His power demonstrated through me. God had told me that I would come to a point where I realized my answer lay only in the Father—not in returning to YWAM, not in finding another career, not even in getting married or getting my money back. I had to choose God and His kingdom, and all that may go with it—including rejection, loneliness and discrimination.

"He has walled me in so I can not go out" (Lam. 3:7). That was Jeremiah's wrong deduction concerning the hard time he was going through. For more than a dozen years, I'd had the confidence every day that even if it was an "evil" day, I was in God's will. All that had changed when I quit preaching and turned my back on the gift God had given me. I had backed myself in a corner, and the fear was ever-present that I wouldn't be able to get out. I had put myself in this predicament.

I took a job setting up appointments for salesmen, but since the salesmen couldn't seem to sell anything, I received no income. I kept refinancing loans and using my new Visa. I had bugged God for so long to let me get a job and live like a normal person, yet now it had all blown up in my face.

A friend told me about some renewal meetings being held in the area, and I planned my work schedule so I could go. At first I had to get past my disdain for the type of praise songs I was forced to sing; all were geared toward corporate worship, and I simply couldn't feel close to God. All the lyrics referred to "we all" being in the river, and I had no idea what they were talking about. The testimonies irked me; you had to wait through several minutes of laughing just to hear people say how happy they were.

It was all very irritating, but if God was in this, I figured it was my only chance at restoring my relationship with Him. But I didn't feel like laughing. I couldn't laugh. What did I have to laugh about? I had failed in my walk with God, quit the ministry and seemingly had no future.

A radio station in Myrtle Beach, South Carolina, offered me a job, but unless they could help me relocate the move was out of the question. A friend who once worked at that station told me they wouldn't have the funds to move me, so I'd might as well forget it. The reality was hitting me hard; I felt "walled in."

By now, I hated Virginia Beach. My memory-makers with Pat Robertson and Benny Hinn seemed like a long-forgotten dream. How did I let myself get so far out of God's will? I continued going to the renewal meetings but didn't stay for prayer. Since I was a minister and couldn't stop the nightmare by praying for myself, what could a lay counselor do for me? They might be worse off than I was.

One morning a ray of sunshine pierced my quiet time, which was usually pretty short if I had one at all. The Lord confirmed to me that I would move to Myrtle Beach and live by the ocean. At that time, the church where the renewal meetings were being held was featuring a ministry at the forefront of the "holy laughter" controversy. I was skeptical; after all, who could trust a man with three names? The first hour I listened to Gil Howard-Browne justify the activity; by the second hour I felt like screaming, *"Fine! Let's see some!"*

Within two minutes of that thought, he ended his talk and walked right over to the aisle I was on. I looked back at him as his eyes locked onto mine. His eyes radiated the most pure love I had ever seen. He started walking toward me. Twelve hundred other pairs of eyes were watching us, but I didn't care. Normally, people would stand up when he came their way for prayer, but I sat there immobilized and melting from the authenticity of God's anointing that was evident in him. Of all the people in the sanctuary, why would he come to one so hard and snarly looking as me? The answer radiated through his shining eyes.

As he reached out and laid his hands on my head, God spoke these words into my spirit: "You are a cherished prize. I want you back." As if a lightning bolt had hit me, I flew off the chair, fell on the floor and cried for at least forty minutes. This was no gentle weeping. It was more like the wailing of a widow— deep, deep moans as if I was grieving for someone who had died.

In fact, someone *had* died—me. As I laid there, oblivious to all that was going on around me, my mind swirled with vivid pictures and thoughts of all the people and situations that had crushed me over the previous couple of years: the leery ministers, the cancellations, the abrupt secretaries and the intense and abysmal loneliness. The loudest cries came as I thought about the twelve years of linking my trust in God's sovereignty to Rev. Doe. It was like an explosion of forgiveness engulfed me. It wasn't that I didn't care that those people had hurt me; it was that it didn't matter anymore. I wanted God back, and apparently He wanted me, too. I could finally say with total conviction: "Put your hope in God, for I will yet praise him, my Savior and my God" (Ps. 43:5).

The following day the evangelist conducted a ministers' meeting. He called me up front, and the same thing happened. I fell over backwards and cried for about a half hour. That night, after Gil finished his message, he again came directly over to my aisle, and his eyes were glued to mine. He had the biggest grin and twinkle in his eyes as he started toward me. I couldn't help but smile myself. I felt happy for the first time in a long time. I stayed seated, and this time, as he put his hand on me, I began to giggle. I didn't know how much of the giggling was spiritual, but I felt light and free, almost giddy. A warmth flooded me, and in a second I found myself on my back, on the floor, laughing. I could hear it, but I wasn't in control of it. The best way to describe it is that I was experiencing complete joy. I was being supernaturally delivered from the oppression of despair, grief and guilt. My spirit and soul had gone from lamentations to ecstasy, and my body responded in tears and with deep laughter. This tearful laughing was such a phenomenon that I knew something unique, genuine and alive had been birthed.

The preacher was relentless. It didn't matter where he was in the room, every time I'd get back in my seat, he'd come back over or just look at me from across the sanctuary and I'd fall on the floor again. I felt revitalized yet exhausted. I didn't want it to stop. The following night I brought a girl who had been ill. She sat across the aisle from me. The last worship song was about God relighting the fire in our hearts. In a flash the guilt of my backslide vanished. If hundreds in that room could sing that song with tears streaming down their faces, then why should I feel like such a failure? Apparently, I wasn't alone.

After the sermon, the preacher again walked over to me after praying for a few people along the way. Excitement and anticipation pulsed through my veins. As he got closer, I pointed to my friend and mouthed, "Pray for her." He didn't even look at her. Laughing, I jumped up, slapped him lightly on the arm and said, "Quit picking on me." He just stared at me with that incredible expression on his face. He laid his hand on my head. I flew six feet backwards onto the floor, but at the time I didn't know it. Apparently, I was there for quite some time laughing and praising God. Guess I was in the river!

I joined a few others up front where the preacher was now softly playing the organ and singing. I surprised myself at the freedom I had to raise my arms and worship God. My eyes were closed, but I knew my face was radiating that same look I'd seen on the speaker's face, one of inexpressible joy. In the wafting of the organ music, I heard "Chris" but didn't even think about it. Certainly he wasn't talking to me. Again I heard, "Chris, look at me." I opened my eyes to see him obviously about to ask me to do something. Now there's one thing I do know, these international ministers never let a stranger do anything at their meetings. That's a "no-no."

He shifted his eyes toward a woman standing up front with about a dozen bodies lying on the floor around her. My first thought as he spoke was, "Don't you dare!" But it was too late. He asked me to go pray for her. I hesitated. "Go Chris. Go now," he said. You could have heard a pin drop as I took those very unsettling steps over to her. What if she doesn't respond? The pressure was on. Has God really forgiven me? Would He still use me? The woman had her eyes closed, her arms raised. She didn't even know I was next to her and that everyone was watching.

I placed my hands on the sides of her head. Poof, she went hurling backwards onto the floor and started laughing. She testified later that she had come two weeks earlier from Ireland. When I touched her, she said she felt electricity enter her. She confessed that she hadn't laughed about anything in a long, long time, but now she was free, and so was I! God had affirmed that I was still valuable to Him and His work. And here

He had done it in front of a number of ministers that had never accepted me. "I thank Christ Jesus our Lord, who has given me strength, that he considered me faithful, appointing me to his service" (1 Tim. 1:12); never were those words as personal to me as they were that night.

Now I was ready for anything God had for me. If He said I was going to Myrtle Beach, then I was sure it would happen. I called the radio station and discovered to my disbelief that they had hired a local person to fill the spot they had offered me seven months earlier.

For the next eight weeks I worked on a book for a man who had left the country temporarily, and although he had paid me some in advance, he was gone now and my bills were due. As glad as I was to be back with God, I wasn't in a hurry to return to all it takes to be a traveling evangelist. I still needed a vision, and I didn't have one. I also felt a bit unsure of my ability to hear from God, since apparently Myrtle Beach was out.

I called Pastor Kurt and invited him out for a Big Mac. As we were digging in to our meal, a man came over to the table. He said he had felt just like I did before the renewal meetings. He and his friends had watched me the first few days. I stood out because of the hardness of my face and my body language. His friends had cried tears of joy as they watched me fly through the air and hit the floor. It was obvious I hadn't faked it. After all, there was no one to catch me! He said my newfound softness and joy proved that God was working in those types of meetings.

Kurt and I went back to our meal, and in mid-sentence he told me to be quiet. "Don't say a word," he said. He closed his eyes. Forty-five seconds later he looked at me and said, "You're leaving here soon." In an instant, he had seen a beach with palm trees. I started refuting him, and he cut me off again. "Shush, be quiet. Chris, a bearded man is going to come into your life."

I didn't know what to say, so I buried it. Over the next weeks, as my heart was healing, little by little the desire to preach again surfaced. But the truth was I wanted a whole new area to minister in. I wanted to start fresh and clean, somewhere new, because that's how I felt. But going out again into ministry would be different this time, because I would be different. It's one thing to testify about how God changed me from a child of Satan to a woman of God, but it was another to tell of how I had unclean lips like Isaiah and had wrestled with God like Jacob.

As a Christian, I had done both. I was unclean in my rebellion and independence; therefore, God had wrestled with me and won. Now, when I went out in His name, what could mere man do to me?

Summer was almost over, and it was too late to get any bookings. Most churches would have their fall schedules filled. I opened the Bible one night to the following scriptures, which were underlined in pink from my days in New Zealand: *"Now begin the work, and the LORD be with you . . . has he not granted you rest on every side? . . . Now devote your heart and soul to seeking the LORD your God,"* (1 Chron. 22:16-19). But that night they had new meaning for me. God was giving me guidance and prophecy.

The bearded man was on his way, but I didn't know it. Within one month everything in my life changed. I received a letter from a man named Richard who lived two hundred miles away and had heard me preach the year before. He felt that God wanted us to meet. I looked up his phone number and called him to scope him out. A week later, Richard came to town. But I had the flu, and that gave me a good excuse not to meet with him. I felt sorry he had come so far, but I had no intention of becoming involved with someone long distance.

He wanted to come over anyway. Reluctantly, I opened the door upon his arrival, and there was Richard with his salt and pepper beard. It seems Richard *and his wife* had been impressed with my ministry at his church and also by my autobiography. His pastor had given him my address, which he filed away and basically forgot about. Over a year later, he remembered me and prayed, asking if it was time for him to contact me. His wife had died only six months earlier, and he wanted to be sure of his motives. That night when he put his watch on the dresser, just like he did every night, there was the piece of paper with my address on it. He figured the time was right.

The result of God bringing us together has been immeasurable; through Richard, I was able to get the healing I needed, as well as rest and peace. God had sent Richard to help me find a spacious, double-wide mobile home surrounded by palm trees—right by the sea in south Myrtle Beach.

There, I was able to lock myself away in the quietness of a beach resort in winter and really learn what it's like to have no one to talk to you in person. Because there was nothing to do and no one to do nothing with, I was able to finish a writing project the Lord had first asked me to do in 1992 as I packed to leave Minneapolis.

I had rest on every side, because I was secure that Richard would finance my writing until the Lord kne v

I was ready to go back into preaching and earn my living from that. I needed months of solitude to really see what was important and what wasn't. The grass was not greener anywhere but in God's will. Richard and I became friends over the phone. He had been alone and bewildered for many months, and God had given him something to ease his pain—helping me!

Thirty-One

Already Married

*"I have loved you with an everlasting love; I have
drawn you with lovingkindness. I will build you up
again and you will be rebuilt."*
—Jeremiah 31:3-4

The above verses parallel the way God sent
"someone to show the way" and how He healed me and
restored me to Himself in such pure love. God had to
build me up again. I didn't think it was possible to go
back to the way I had been. I thought the essence of
who I was in Christ was gone. What wasn't left in
Minneapolis was now, over time, strewn up and down
the East Coast.

I felt I had come to the end of me, which is exactly
what God wanted, but preaching it is one thing and
surrendering to it is another. I knew I couldn't return
to ministry until all the battle wounds had been tended
to and my thought life had been drastically altered. My

problem wasn't that I didn't want to preach anymore. But I had questions: *Who am I to preach anyway? What would my message be now if I couldn't even follow the lessons in my own sermons?*

In the restoration process, I experienced a complete paradigm shift in my understanding of grace and mercy, and with that, my trust and hope in God returned. I realized how amazing His grace was to save me in the first place, then to maneuver me into YWAM where I could be discipled and, for a season of several years, have the best friendships of my life. That was mercy. He knew I wouldn't have made it in the church I had been attending in Hawaii. I had to feel wanted in this new kingdom I had entered.

It was there that God intoxicated me with the work of an evangelist so that I would see my purpose and never want to stop, but when my "I quit" tape clicked on fourteen years later, I became like David. He had a "Why bother?" attitude too. When it was time for kings to go to war, he stayed home. It was then that he turned to other things. I too got involved with futile things because I had left the battle, but God knew that I would eventually appreciate Him with a new awareness. He provided a beautiful place for me to relearn the lesson of His mercy and grace that will be extended even to those who, like David, had a heart after Him but shelved it for a while and went striving after the wind.

Yes, getting saved was one thing but receiving His forgiveness and mercy again, after my *meshubah*, that too was a miracle.

Upon my arrival in Myrtle Beach, in my first guilt-free quiet time in a while, God brought two revelations to me, both for comfort and for prophecy, using the story in Acts 28 in which Paul is among those shipwrecked on the island of Malta. I had read this chapter many times before, of course, but this time God used this section of Scripture to provide both light and closure to my long ordeal.

Despite all the things thrown my way over the years, I should have remained steadfast, immovable, abounding in the work of the Lord. Instead I let the offenses build up. What God wanted me to learn was that with the steady stream of bummers I'd dealt with, I should be ready for anything. I should get to the point that no matter what negative thing attaches itself to me, I shouldn't let it faze me.

me too

Notice in Acts 28:3 that a viper goes right for Paul, fastening onto his hand with a poisonous bite. Does Paul jump up and down, freaking out? No, he remains steadfast as a result of all his trials. Paul simply shakes the snake off. God not only wanted me to shake off the feelings and thought life from my *meshubah,* He also wanted to warn me that the enemy would try to slither in again. The more times I shake him off, the easier and more automatic it will become.

God then reminded me of a vision I'd had at a really low point, a time when I had reflected on the good years I'd had with God but concluded that the best was over.

In the vision I was sitting in a large theater with the lights on. No one else was around. The curtain was closed on the stage, yet I was reading the program. My first thought was, *The play's over, and I still don't know what it was about. And as usual, there's no one here for me to ask.* But the Lord spoke. *"It's not over,"* He said. He explained the vision: *"You're reading the program before the play has begun, not after it's over."*

That vision was given for an appointed time, and Myrtle Beach was it.

"For your Maker is your husband—the LORD Almighty is his name" (Is. 54:5). How many times over the years had this verse brought comfort and security? How many times had I seen the truth and reality of it? Getting me to Myrtle Beach brought a greater revelation of the covenant I had entered into when I got saved.

I had become His bride. And all that a husband is required to do, God himself would do for me—love, honor and cherish in sickness and in health, for richer or for poorer, and in death!

In Genesis 15 God makes a promise to Abraham about his future and his inheritance. Abraham asks, "O Sovereign LORD, how can I know that I will gain possession of it?" (verse 8). God tells him specifically what sort of sacrifice he is to make, and then God makes a covenant with him.

The explicit and special sacrifice that Abraham makes had the same effect as a notary stamping a contract. Once done, it was binding. In the same way, Jesus shed His blood sacrificially to make a new and binding covenant with believers.

With binding covenants and contracts in mind let's look at the institution of marriage. What a perfect picture that paints of our binding relationship with God.

"Then I passed by you and saw you, and behold, you were at the time for love; so I spread My skirt over you and covered your nakedness. I also swore to you and entered into a covenant with you so that you became Mine" (Ez. 16:8, NAS). When I was only a few weeks old in the faith, during a quiet time the reference to this

portion of Scripture was spoken in my heart. I went to the table of contents in my Bible to find it. As I began to read the above words for the first time, the power behind them was physically evident within me.

I trembled and then cried.

The words have become alive to me again. Just as God drew me to His Son the first time, because I belong to him He drew me back again. In both cases, I was "at the time for love."

In the Old Testament, the wedding day was the most important day in a person's life, especially for the bride. Many believed it was for that day she had come into the world, and great preparation was taken in bringing the bride and groom together. The girl waited in anticipation, even though it was very likely she would not even meet her intended husband till the wedding day. The father controlled this decision and her future.

But the choice of the bride was in the hands of the groom's father. He would search for the perfect choice for his son and then buy her. A contract was made and goods were promised or exchanged, to show that she was worthy and valuable to the father's son. After all, she would help to increase his family.

It was her responsibility to learn all she could that would please her husband-to-be—and to keep herself pure and spotless for the wedding day, which could be years away. The son was to return to the father's house to begin to prepare a place for her, so that some day she could be there with him.

When the son's father determined it was the right time for the two to be married, he sent someone out ahead of his son to blow a horn, loud enough to be heard from afar, indicating that the time had arrived.

Get ready—the groom is coming for his bride! At the sound, she begins her final preparations. She cleanses herself with perfumed water and gathers her white wedding dress. In effect, she is saying, "I am as pure and clean as the snow."

She returns with the groom, ready to come under the authority of the father. It doesn't matter what she got away with at home; some things simply won't fly anymore.

A family celebration begins, and then the couple go into the bridal chamber while everyone waits for the verdict: Had she been faithful? The announcement is made: "Yes, she had"—there is proof on the bed sheet. The rabbi then puts his mark on the cloth, sealing this truth, so no one can ever accuse her of not being loyal, dedicated and committed. The marriage was now binding, and the son could not discard her as long as she honored the covenant of marriage.

Now if she had not been faithful at the time of the blowing of the horn, she could go directly to the father, make her confession, attest to her repentance and ask for mercy. This had to be done before the wedding night or else the contract was null and void, and she was stoned to death!

She would lay at the father's feet and ask for forgiveness. It was his choice and his choice alone if she could stay. He was still the one who would decide who his son's bride would be, but he knows how long it took to find her. He knows what it cost to buy her, and he knows that even though she has sinned, she is still valuable—for she had been chosen a long time ago.

And so have you.

"He does not treat us as our sins deserve or repay us according to our iniquities" (Ps. 103:10). How many times did individual Israelites slide away and find themselves with a different heart? After trying to get out on their own, they eventually called upon the Father to save them, and He did!

You and I both know that someday when the Father, and only the Father, decides the time is right to collect the bride, we will hear a trumpet and go to the place that has been prepared for us.

If you have been unfaithful to the Lord—for whatever reason and in whatever manner—it's time to make your peace with the Father. The brides-to-be in Old Testament times had their chance when they heard the horn. But as you know, when the trumpet sounds for Christ's return, we won't have the benefit of that aspect of the wedding rite.

If you have a weary heart or a wounded spirit, if you are laboring under the grief of deferred hope, I want you to know that you are not alone. More importantly, I want you to understand that you can come back. For me, it was a long time from the day I cried out in the car until the time I knew I was restored and had matured. My message to others, in and out of the pulpit, will never be the same.

You have not gone too far. You are still betrothed, and the covenant is still binding. But the trumpet is about to blow.

What do you think your heavenly Father's words to you will be when you lay at His feet and ask forgiveness? He chose you to be betrothed to His Son. He chose you before the foundations of the world. You have long since been paid for. You are still valuable to Him.

227

Let God speak to your *my* weary heart! He will not forget you. He will not abandon you. These are His words to you: "I remember the devotion of your youth, how as a bride you loved me and followed me through the desert, through a land not sown" (Jer. 2:2).

You, my friend, are priceless to the Father. Come back and do not only the deeds you once did but go forward with new deeds, with a renewed, soft heart.